WOK

WOK

hamlyn

Published in the UK in 1998
by Hamlyn, a division of Octopus Publishing Group Ltd
2–4 Heron Quays, London E14 4JP

This edition published 2002 by Octopus Publishing Group Ltd

Copyright ©1998, 2002 Octopus Publishing Group Ltd

ISBN 0 600 60829 8

Printed in China

NOTES

Both metric and imperial measurements have been given in all
recipes. Use one set of measurements only and not a
mixture of both.

Standard level spoon measurements are used in all recipes.
1 tablespoon = one 15 ml spoon
1 teaspoon = one 5 ml spoon

Eggs should be medium to large unless otherwise stated.
The Department of Health advises that eggs should not be
consumed raw. This book contains dishes made with raw or
lightly cooked eggs. It is prudent for more vulnerable people
such as pregnant and nursing mothers, invalids, the elderly,
babies and young children to avoid uncooked or lightly cooked
dishes made with eggs. Once prepared, these dishes should
be kept refrigerated and used promptly.

All meat and poultry should be thoroughly cooked before serving.

Milk should be full fat unless otherwise stated.

Do not re-freeze a dish that has been frozen previously.

Pepper should be freshly ground black pepper unless
otherwise stated.

Fresh herbs should be used, unless otherwise stated. If
unavailable, use dried herbs as an alternative but halve the
quantities stated.

Measurements for canned food have been given as a standard
metric equivalent.

Nuts and nut derivatives
This book includes dishes made with nuts and nut derivatives.
It is advisable for customers with known allergic reactions to
nuts and nut derivatives and those who may be potentially
vulnerable to these allergies, such as pregnant and nursing
mothers, invalids, the elderly, babies and children, to avoid
dishes made with nuts and nut oils. It is also prudent to check
the labels of pre-prepared ingredients for the possible inclusion
of nut derivatives.

Ovens should be preheated to the specified temperature – if
using a fan-assisted oven, follow the manufacturer's
instructions for adjusting the time and the temperature.

Contents

Introduction

A curved pan made famous by popular Chinese cooking, the wok is used all over South-East Asia, in Thai, Indonesian, Malaysian and Vietnamese cooking. Authentically, thin and made of carbon-steel, a wok is designed for use over a fierce brazier. The rounded base fits neatly into a simple stand over an open flame and the deep sides allow experienced cooks to shake and toss ingredients with acrobatic skill. This type of performance is given by street chefs on food stalls all over Malaysia, as they toss and flip ingredients with incredible skill, often over alarmingly high flames. For the home cook, a wok can be just as exciting and perfectly practical.

BUYING A WOK

In the average western kitchen a wok will be used on a gas or electric hob, so the majority of designs have a slightly flattened base. Ring stands can be bought for completely curved woks; these can be used on gas hobs, usually by placing them over the burner instead of the usual pan support, but the small area of hob top between the burner and the ring becomes heavily soiled during cooking.

Look for a steeply curved wok which has deep sides and a lid, also check the type of material from which it is made or any coating on it. Some woks can be difficult to keep clean while others can

conveniently be put in the dishwasher.
• Carbon steel is practical only if the wok is in constant use as it has to be scrubbed with salt and oiled. This type of wok is ideal for stir-frying as the metal conducts heat well, quickly becoming hot, but if sauces or foods stick during cooking and the wok is washed, it has to be seasoned thoroughly by heating with oil and wiping out. Even when coated with oil and stored in polythene, this type of wok will rust if not used frequently.
• Stainless steel can be used over a high heat and stands up to stir-frying well. It is also excellent for braising and steaming. A good-quality wok of this type usually has a slightly flattened base for use on electric or gas hobs; it is washable and will last for years.
• Non-stick finishes are popular and practical but they are not intended for use over fierce heat, which can be a disadvantage for extremely rapid stir-frying, and manufacturers often recommend that they should not be heated empty, without any oil or food. Nevertheless, this is often a more practical choice than carbon steel. Buy suitable utensils for use with non-stick surfaces to avoid scratching them.

ACCESSORIES

Wok sets often include spatulas or scoop-shaped spoons which can be

used for tossing and turning ingredients or serving them when cooked. Extra long chopsticks, or cooking chopsticks, are useful for stir-frying food or swirling ingredients together, for example when making soup.

Many woks are packaged with some form of rack for briefly steaming food. This looks rather like a round cooling rack for baking and it can be placed over a small amount of water in the bottom of the wok. If you do not have a steaming rack, a round wire cooling rack is an excellent substitute.

A draining rack is also sometimes included for use when deep-frying. This small rack hooks over the side, providing a narrow `shelf' on the inside of the pan on which to place freshly fried food, allowing oil to drip back into the wok.

Bamboo steamers can be stacked in a wok. Small steamers look fun, but those with a larger diameter are more practical. Check that the steamer is neither too large to sit neatly inside the wok nor too small to allow a good depth of water to be poured in underneath it. Most bamboo steamer sets come with two layers and a lid but additional layers can be purchased.

TECHNIQUES

A wok is ideal for speedy stir-frying, steaming or short braising. Traditionally, a wok is also used for deep-frying food, but it is not sufficiently stable for cooking in any great depth of oil.

BOILING

Unless you intend thoroughly seasoning it with oil, inside and out, a carbon steel wok is not ideal to use for boiling. Small amounts of noodles or other oriental pasta can be softened in simmering water, but a saucepan is more practical for cooking a large portion or for items that require longer cooking.

Soups can be prepared in the wok as there is ample room for four portions or six modest servings. The width of the pan makes it ideal for preparing Egg Drop Soup (see page 16) as there is plenty of surface area into which the beaten egg can be swirled.

DEEP-FRYING

A wok is practical for deep-frying small amounts of food; but do not use more than a shallow depth of oil. The level rises when the oil is heated and food is added, so cook ingredients in small batches. Always ensure food is dried well to prevent oil from spitting.

MAKING CRISPY RICE

This applies particularly to Crispy Rice with Dipping Sauce (page 79).

Spread some drained boiled rice out in a thin layer on greased baking sheets. Press down well and leave to dry for several hours, either in a warm place or a cool oven 120°C (250°F), Gas Mark ½.

When completely dry and firm, remove the rice from the baking sheets with a spatula and break into pieces about 7–10 cm (3–4 inches) across.

Half-fill a wok or large frying pan with vegetable oil and heat until very hot. Drop in some of the rice pieces. Deep-fry until golden. Remove the cooked rice pieces from the oil with a slotted spoon and drain on kitchen paper. Repeat with the remaining rice pieces in batches. Serve the crispy rice with a dipping sauce (see page 79).

STEAMING

Food can be steamed on a rack over a little water in the base of the wok. This is ideal for foil-wrapped food, like fish or vegetables, or food can be steamed in a shallow dish or on a plate. Alternatively, a bamboo steamer can be placed over the wok. To prevent ingredients sticking, line a bamboo steamer with cabbage leaves. A wok holds enough water for short periods of steaming; check the level during cooking and top up with boiling water if necessary.

STIR-BRAISING

This often follows on from stir-frying, when liquid is added to the briefly cooked ingredients. The ingredients are simmered gently for a short period and stirred frequently during cooking.

STIR-FRYING

Stir-frying is rapid cooking over a high, or fairly high heat in a small amount of oil, stirring the food continuously. The curved shape and large surface area in a wok is ideal for this, allowing food to be tossed and turned as it is cooked.

When cooking a variety of ingredients together, add them in stages, starting with the foods that require the most cooking. For example, for pork with vegetables, stir-fry the pork briefly, then add the vegetables in order, starting with those requiring longest cooking, carrots or celery perhaps, and ending with ingredients needing only brief cooking, such as beansprouts.

PREPARING INGREDIENTS

Since wok cookery is relatively quick, tender ingredients should be used and for rapid cooking methods they should be cut finely and evenly. Stir-frying is the most popular method and even when it is complemented by brief braising or stir-braising before the food is served, the overall cooking time does not allow tough meats or chunky vegetables to become tender.

BUTTERFLY PRAWNS

This is a decorative preparation method for large uncooked prawns. Peel the prawns, leaving the tail in place, then split them almost through along the back and flatten them. Their shape will then resemble a butterfly.

CUTTING FINE STRIPS

First cut thin slices, then stack several slices together and cut them across into fine strips.

Cut vegetables like carrots into short lengths, stand these on end and slice them vertically, holding the slices firmly together, then give the entire piece a quarter turn and slice it vertically again, allowing the fine strips to fall away as they are sliced.

CUTTING FISH STRIPS

Fish fillets can be cut into strips which cook well with stir-fried vegetables. The strips should not be as fine as poultry, meat or vegetables or they will fall apart during cooking. Skin the fillets, if liked, and cut them across to form strips. Dust with flour or, for most oriental cuisines, cornflour before cooking.

PREPARING UNCOOKED PRAWNS

Raw prawns are available peeled and ready to cook or in their shells. To peel prawns, break off the head and tail shell. Holding the underneath of the shell uppermost, break it sideways with your thumbs. When the thin shell is broken underneath it slips off easily leaving the tail meat intact. Use a cocktail stick to pick out the thin dark vein running along the back of the tail.

SHREDDING

To shred leaves, roll them into a neat bundle and finely slice with a sharp knife.

To shred white or red cabbage, first cut the heads into slim wedges. Trim off any thick area of tough stalk, then slice the wedge across thinly and the slices will separate into shreds as they are cut.

SLICING POULTRY OR MEAT

Boneless pieces of frying or roasting cuts of meat and breast fillets of poultry are suitable. Trim off any skin and fat. Cut thin slices across the grain as these cook quickly giving tender results.

SLICING SPRING ONIONS

Spring onions are usually cut into long slices at an angle, resulting in a cut that is halfway between a slice and a strip. Cut at a sharp angle making slices that are 2.5–5 cm (1–2 inches) in width and very thin.

SLICING VEGETABLES

Vegetables, such as carrots, stir-fry well when sliced at an angle. This makes a slightly oval shape and gives a larger surface area so that the slices cook quickly. Cut at an acute slant, making long, thin slices.

SPRING ONION TASSELS

Trim off most of the green top and the root of a spring onion. Then finely shred the short section of green, leaving the shreds attached at the base. If preferred, the spring onion can be shredded from both ends, leaving the pieces attached by a short section in the middle. Place in a bowl of iced water and leave for about 30 minutes, until the shreds have curled.

BASIC INGREDIENTS

CHICKEN STOCK

This recipe makes a good amount of stock. It can be stored in an air-tight container in the refrigerator for up to 3 days. If you prefer, it can be made in advance and frozen; it will keep in the freezer for up to 3 months.

1 Put a 1 kg/2 lb chicken (giblets reserved) in a large saucepan with 2.5 litres/4 pints water. Add the giblets (except the liver which would make the stock taste bitter), 1 onion and 1 carrot, both quartered, 1–2 celery sticks, sliced, 1 large bouquet garni, 6 black peppercorns and a pinch of salt. Bring to the boil, skimming off the scum as it rises to the surface.

2 Lower the heat, half cover the pan and simmer gently for 3 hours. Skim and top up the water as necessary.

3 Remove the bird and strain the stock into a bowl. Blot off any surface fat with kitchen paper and use as needed.

FISH STOCK

This stock is quick to prepare and well worth making for its extra flavour. Do not cook it for longer than the time stated, or it will taste bitter. It can be kept in an air-tight container for up to 24 hours in the refrigerator. If you prefer, it can be made in advance and frozen; it will keep in the freezer for up to 3 months.

1 Put 500 g/1 lb fish trimmings (heads, bones, skin etc.) into a saucepan with 900 ml/1½ pints water, 2 tablespoons chopped onion, 2 tablespoons chopped celery, a handful of parsley, 2 bay leaves, 1 teaspoon black peppercorns and 2–3 tablespoons dry white wine.

2 Bring slowly to the boil, skim off any scum forming on the surface. Half cover the pan and simmer for 25 minutes.

3 Strain the stock through a fine sieve and use as required.

VEGETABLE STOCK

Another quickly made stock, this stock can be kept in an air-tight container for up to 3 days in the refrigerator. If you prefer, it can be made in advance and frozen; it will keep in the freezer for up to 3 months.

1 Heat 4 tablespoons of sunflower oil in a heavy-based saucepan. Add 2 garlic cloves, 2 chopped onions and 2 sliced leeks. Fry gently for 10 minutes.

2 Add 2 diced potatoes, 4 chopped carrots and 4 sliced celery sticks. Fry for a further 10 minutes.

3 Add 4 chopped ripe tomatoes to the saucepan with 125 g/4 oz mushrooms, 125 g/4 oz rice, a bouquet garni and 1.8 litres/3 pints water. Bring to the boil and simmer for 30 minutes.

4 Strain the stock through a fine sieve and use as required.

COCONUT MILK AND CREAM

Coconut milk is not the liquid inside a fresh coconut. It comes from the flesh of the coconut, infused in hot water. If the coconut 'milk' is left to stand, a thicker 'cream' rises to the top. Both coconut milk and cream are readily available in supermarkets and Oriental stores.

To make your own, mix 900 ml/ 1½ pints water and 400 g/13 oz grated or desiccated coconut in a saucepan. Bring the mixture to the boil, lower the heat and simmer, stirring occasionally, until the mixture is reduced by one-third. Strain, squeezing out as much liquid as possible. Pour the strained milk into a bowl and chill in the refrigerator. When it is cold, skim off the thicker cream that has risen to the surface.

GARLIC MIXTURE

This mixture is used in many recipes in this book. Although best when fresh, it can be made in advance and stored in an air-tight container in the refrigerator for up to 2 days.

Place 2 tablespoons crushed garlic, 2 tablespoons chopped coriander root or stem and ½ tablespoon pepper in a blender or food processor and grind to a paste. Alternatively, pound in a mortar with a pestle.

TAMARIND WATER

Tamarind is the sticky brown pulp of the seed pod of the tamarind tree and is sold as a paste in blocks.

To make Tamarind Water, dilute some tamarind paste in 4 times its quantity of water. Bring the water to simmering point, and break up the paste in the water. Leave to cool, then strain through a sieve, pressing through as much of the paste as possible to give a thick liquid.

SERVING

A bright, attractive wok can be an exciting serving pan, especially when preparing one-pot meals, like Chow Mein (see page 80). Make sure that you have a heatproof base on which to stand the wok securely. Resting it in a wide shallow dish on a cork mat can make the wok more stable.

Basic Recipes

Thai Red Curry Paste

- 6 dried red chillies, deseeded, soaked and roughly chopped
- 2 tablespoons chopped lemon grass
- 1 teaspoon chopped coriander root or stem
- 1 tablespoon chopped shallots
- 1 tablespoon chopped garlic
- 1 teaspoon chopped galangal
- 2 teaspoons coriander seeds
- 1 teaspoon cumin seeds
- 6 white peppercorns
- 1 teaspoon salt
- 1 teaspoon shrimp paste

1 Put all the curry paste ingredients in a blender or food processor and grind to a thick paste.

2 Alternatively, put the chillies in a mortar and crush with a pestle, then add the lemon grass and crush it with the coriander, and so on with all the other ingredients.

3 Transfer the paste to an airtight container and store in the refrigerator for up to 3 weeks.

Preparation time: 15 minutes

Thai Yellow Curry Paste

- 2.5 cm/1 inch galangal, finely chopped
- 1 lemon grass stalk, finely chopped
- 2 shallots, chopped
- 3 garlic cloves, chopped
- 2 teaspoons turmeric
- 1 teaspoon ground coriander
- 1 teaspoon ground cumin
- 1 teaspoon shrimp paste
- ½ teaspoon chilli powder

1 Put all the curry paste ingredients in a blender or food processor and grind to a thick paste.

2 Alternatively, put the galangal in a mortar and crush with a pestle, then add the lemon grass and crush it with the shallots, and so on with all the other ingredients.

3 Transfer the paste to an airtight container and store in the refrigerator for up to 3 weeks.

Preparation time: 15 minutes

Thai Green Curry Paste

- 15 small green chillies
- 4 garlic cloves, halved
- 2 lemon grass stalks, finely chopped
- 2 lime leaves, torn
- 2 shallots, chopped
- 50 g/2 oz coriander leaves, stalks and roots
- 2.5 cm/1 inch root ginger, peeled and chopped
- 2 teaspoons coriander seeds
- 1 teaspoon black peppercorns
- 1 teaspoon finely grated lime, rind
- ½ teaspoon salt
- 2 tablespoons groundnut oil

1 Put all the curry paste ingredients in a blender or food processor and grind to a thick paste.

2 Alternatively, put the chillies in a mortar and crush with the pestle, then add the garlic and crush it with the lemon grass, and so on with all the other ingredients, finally mixing in the oil with a spoon.

3 Transfer the paste to an airtight container and store in the refrigerator for up to 3 weeks.

Preparation time: 15 minutes

Soups and Starters

A wok is ideal for simmering perfect Egg Drop Soup or a satisfying broth with tasty wontons – both excellent first courses or ideal for light meals. Deep-fried Corn Cakes or crispy Vietnamese Spring Rolls will whet the appetite. Arrange them with other irresistible savouries on a buffet platter for an informal supper or as party fare.

Crispy Seaweed

Preparation time: 10 minutes, plus drying
Cooking time: 10 minutes

- 750 g (1½ lb) spring greens
- vegetable oil for deep-frying
- 1½ teaspoons caster sugar
- 1 teaspoon salt

1 Separate the leaves of the spring greens. Wash them well and then pat dry with kitchen paper or a clean tea-towel.

2 Using a very sharp knife, shred the spring greens into the thinnest possible shavings. Spread out the shreds on kitchen paper and leave for about *30 minutes*, until thoroughly dry.

3 In a wok, heat the oil for deep-frying to 180–190°C (350–375°F), or until a cube of bread browns in *30 seconds*. Turn off the heat for *30 seconds*, then add a small batch of spring green shreds. Turn up the heat to moderate and deep-fry the greens until they begin to float. Take care as they tend to spit while they are cooking.

4 Remove the greens with a slotted spoon and drain them on kitchen paper. Cook the remaining greens in batches in the same way. When they are all cooked, transfer to a bowl and sprinkle with the sugar and salt. Toss gently to mix and serve warm or cold.

Serves 8

Egg Drop Soup

This widely known Chinese soup is easily prepared and the wok is ideal for doing this because it gives a large surface area of soup into which the beaten egg can be swirled. The success of this soup depends on the quality of the stock, so don't try to cut corners by using a cube.

Preparation time: 15 minutes
Cooking time: 5–7 minutes

- 900 ml (1½ pints) Chicken Stock (see page 9)
- 10 spring onions
- 2 tablespoons chopped fresh coriander leaves
- about 4 tablespoons soy sauce
- 2 teaspoons cornflour
- 1 tablespoon cold water
- 2 eggs
- salt and pepper

1 Prepare the stock according to the recipe instructions, straining it and skimming off any excess fat if necessary. Stir in the chopped chicken meat that was used to make the stock. Chop 6 of the spring onions and mix them with the coriander.

2 Pour the stock into a wok and heat through, then stir in the soy sauce, tasting the soup as you do so, and add seasoning to taste. The soup will need some pepper but, depending on the strength of the soy sauce, it may not need any salt. Blend the cornflour with the water and stir this into the hot soup, then bring it to the boil to thicken slightly.

3 Beat the eggs thoroughly without allowing them to become frothy – the idea is to combine the yolks and whites evenly. Stir the spring onion mixture into the soup, bring to a rapid boil and stir the soup so that it swirls around vigorously in the wok. Immediately turn off the heat and pour in the egg in a slow thin stream. It should set in the swirling soup to give thin strips. Serve immediately, garnished with the 4 remaining spring onions, shredded.

Serves 4

Wonton Soup

Preparation time: 20 minutes
Cooking time: 7–8 minutes

- 175 g (6 oz) minced pork
- 125 g (4 oz) spinach leaves, chopped
- ½ teaspoon salt
- 1 teaspoon sugar
- 1 tablespoon dry sherry
- 24 wonton wrappers (see page 58)
- 900 ml (1½ pints) clear Chicken Stock (see page 9)
- 4–6 chives, snipped, to garnish

1 To make the filling for the wontons, thoroughly mix the minced pork with the spinach, salt, sugar and sherry.

2 Lay the wonton wrappers on a lightly floured surface and place a teaspoonful of the filling in the centre of each.

3 Bring the opposite corners of each wrapper together over the filling and firmly pinch the top edges together to seal them. Fold the other two corners together and seal them in the same way.

4 Bring the stock to the boil in a wok. Drop the wontons into the stock and boil rapidly for *2–3 minutes*. Serve the soup immediately, garnished with snipped chives.

Serves 4–6

Bean Thread Noodle Soup

Preparation time: 10 minutes
Cooking time: 10 minutes

- 2 tablespoons vegetable oil
- 2 teaspoons Garlic Mixture
  (see page 9)
- 250 g (8 oz) minced pork
- 1 litre (1¾ pints) Chicken
  Stock (see page 9)
- 125 g (4 oz) bean thread
  noodles
- 4 spring onions, cut into
  2.5 cm (1 inch) lengths

- ½ onion, finely chopped
- 2 tablespoons *nam pla* (fish
  sauce)
- 2 tablespoons salt
- 250 g (8 oz) uncooked
  prawns, peeled and
  deveined (see page 8)
- 2 celery sticks with leaves,
  sliced
- pepper

1 Heat the oil in a wok, add the Garlic Mixture and stir-fry for
1 minute.

2 Add the minced pork and stir-fry for *3 minutes*, then pour in
the stock and bring to the boil. Stir in the noodles, spring
onions, onion, *nam pla* and salt. Bring the soup back to the
boil and cook for *3 minutes*. Lower the heat, add the prawns
and celery and simmer for a further *2 minutes*.

3 Transfer to a warm serving bowl, season with pepper and
serve immediately

Serves 4

Egg Nets with Pork and Prawn Filling

Preparation time: 10 minutes
Cooking time: 20 minutes

- 6 eggs, lightly beaten
- 2 red chillies, deseeded and sliced into thin strips
- 4 tablespoons torn fresh coriander leaves
- Tangy Chilli Sauce (see page 25), to serve (optional)

FILLING:

- 3 tablespoons vegetable oil
- 1 tablespoon Garlic Mixture (see page 9)
- 250 g (8 oz) minced pork
- 125 g (4 oz) uncooked prawns, peeled, deveined (see page 8) and minced

- 2 tablespoons finely chopped onion
- 3 tablespoons *nam pla* (fish sauce)
- 3 tablespoons sugar
- 125 g (4 oz) roasted peanuts, coarsely chopped

GARNISH:

- ½ red pepper, cored, deseeded and
- ½ green pepper, cored, deseeded and thinly sliced

1 First prepare the filling. Heat 2 tablespoons of the oil in a wok, add the Garlic Mixture and stir-fry for *1 minute*. Add the pork and stir-fry for *5–7 minutes*, then add all the remaining ingredients except the peanuts and cook, stirring, for *3 minutes*. Remove the pan from the heat, mix in the peanuts and set aside.

2 Brush a clean wok with some of the remaining oil and place it over moderate heat. Fit a 5 mm (¼ inch) nozzle into a piping bag and spoon a little of the beaten egg mixture into the bag, keeping the nozzle stopped with a finger. Holding the bag over the wok, remove your finger and drizzle the egg into the centre of the wok in a flat square lattice, measuring about 9 cm (3½ inches) square.

3 As soon as the egg lattice is cooked, slide it on to a plate and keep it warm. Continue to make egg lattices until all the egg mixture has been used, brushing the wok with more oil as necessary.

4 To make the nets, make a cross from 2 pieces of chilli in the centre of each egg lattice square. Place a coriander leaf on top of the chilli and add a heaped teaspoon of the prepared filling.

5 Carefully fold the egg lattice over the filling to form a parcel shape. Repeat with the remaining lattice shapes and filling. Arrange the nets on a serving platter in such a way that the red of the chilli and the green of the coriander can clearly be seen. Serve immediately, garnished with red and green pepper strips, with Tangy Chilli Sauce, if liked.

Serves 4

Deep-fried Corn Cakes

These corn cakes are a popular Thai snack, often served at cocktail parties.

Preparation time: 20 minutes
Cooking time: 8–10 minutes

- 500 g (1 lb) corn on the cob
- 500 g (1 lb) minced pork (not too lean)
- 1 tablespoon Garlic Mixture (see page 9)
- 2 eggs, beaten
- 2 tablespoons plain flour
- 1 tablespoon cornflour
- 1 teaspoon salt
- 2 tablespoons light soy sauce

- ½ vegetable stock cube, crumbled (optional)
- 2 tablespoons chopped fresh coriander leaves, to garnish
- oil for deep-frying

TO SERVE:

- 1 large cucumber, very finely sliced
- 2 red chillies, deseeded and sliced into thin strips

1 Working over a mixing bowl, slice all the kernels off the corn cobs with a sharp knife. Add the pork and Garlic Mixture and mix well, then stir in half of the beaten egg.

2 Add the flours, salt and soy sauce, stirring well to make a mixture which is firm enough to be shaped. If necessary, add more beaten egg. Break off a small piece of the mixture and test fry in a little oil. If it tastes too bland, mix in the half vegetable stock cube.

3 Form the mixture into round flat cakes, each about 3 cm (1½ inches) across. Heat the oil in a wok to 180–190°C (350–375°F), or until a cube of bread browns in *30 seconds*, and deep-fry the cakes, a few at a time, until golden brown. Set aside to drain on kitchen paper and allow to cool.

4 When cool, arrange the corn cakes on a serving plate and garnish with chopped coriander. Serve with cucumber slices and red chilli strips.

Serves 4

Crispy Vegetables

Preparation time: 20 minutes
Cooking time: 2–3 minutes each batch

- 500 g (1 lb) mixed vegetables
  – for example, cauliflower,
  beans, mushrooms,
  mangetout and peppers – cut
  into small pieces
- vegetable oil for deep-frying

AVOCADO DIP:
- 1–2 garlic cloves, roughly
  chopped
- 1 shallot, roughly chopped
- 4 tomatoes, skinned
  deseeded and chopped
- 1 teaspoon chilli powder

- 2 avocados, stoned and
  peeled
- 1 tablespoon chopped fresh
  coriander leaves or a pinch
  of ground coriander
- 1 tablespoon lime or lemon
  juice

BATTER:
- 125 g (4 oz) plain flour
- pinch of salt
- 1 tablespoon vegetable oil
- 150 ml (¼ pint) water
- 2 egg whites

1 Purée the dip ingredients in a food processor or blender until smooth. Alternatively, mash the avocados with a fork and stir in the remaining ingredients. If making the dip by hand, the garlic, shallot and tomatoes should be finely chopped. Spoon the dip into a serving dish, cover with clingfilm and chill for no more than *30 minutes*.

2 To make the batter, sift the flour and salt into a bowl, then gradually beat in the oil and water. Whisk the egg whites until stiff, then fold them into the batter. Heat the oil in a wok to 180–190°C (350–375°F) or until a cube of bread browns in *30 seconds*.

3 Dip the vegetables into the batter, then deep-fry them in batches for *2–3 minutes* each, until golden brown. Remove with a slotted spoon and set aside to drain on kitchen paper. Serve warm with the avocado dip.

Serves 4

Vietnamese Chicken Spring Rolls

Spring rolls are the most popular dish in Vietnamese cuisine, for both rich and poor. They are usually filled with pork and crab, but a combination of any meat or seafood may be used. Cooked spring rolls can be frozen, then reheated in the oven. Alternatively, they can be partially cooked, refrigerated for up to 1 day and the cooking completed before serving. Serve these as an appetizer with a bowl of Tangy Chilli Sauce (see opposite). For a main course, serve with a green salad and offer the sauce separately in individual bowls as a dip.

Preparation time: 40 minutes, plus soaking
Cooking time: about 5 minutes each batch

- 4 eggs, beaten
- 20 rice paper spring roll wrappers
- vegetable oil for deep-frying
- Tangy Chilli Sauce (see opposite), to serve

FILLING:
- 50 g (2 oz) bean thread noodles, soaked in water for *10 minutes*

- 2 dried shiitake mushrooms, soaked in hot water for *30 minutes*
- 500 g (1 lb) boneless, skinless chicken breast, cut into thin strips
- 3 garlic cloves, finely chopped
- 3 shallots, finely chopped
- 250 g (8 oz) crab meat, canned or frozen
- ½ teaspoon pepper

1 Drain the bean thread noodles, then cut them into 2.5 cm (1 inch) pieces. Drain and finely chop the mushrooms, discarding any tough stems.

2 Combine the noodles, mushrooms, chicken, garlic, shallots, crab meat and pepper in a bowl, then mix well with a spoon. Divide the mixture into 20 portions and shape each into a small cylinder.

3 To assemble a spring roll, brush beaten egg over the entire surface of a rice paper wrapper. Leave the paper for a few seconds until it is soft and flexible. Place a portion of the filling near the curved edge of the paper and roll both filling and wrapping once. Then fold over the sides of the paper to enclose the filling and continue rolling. The beaten egg holds the wrapper together. Repeat with the remaining rice paper wrappers and filling.

4 Heat the oil in a wok to 180–190°C (350–375°F), or until a cube of bread browns in *30 seconds*, and deep-fry about one-third of the spring rolls over a moderate heat until golden brown. Remove the rolls from the oil with a slotted spoon and set aside to drain on kitchen paper. Fry the remaining spring rolls in the same way. Serve hot or at room temperature with Tangy Chilli Sauce.

Makes 20 rolls

Tangy Chilli Sauce

This hot, tangy Vietnamese sauce is sprinkled on food as required as well as being used in many recipes. Tangy Chilli Sauce can be made in larger quantities and kept in the refrigerator for up to 1 week. Store the sauce in a glass jar with a tightly fitting lid.

Preparation time: *10 minutes*

- 2 garlic cloves
- 4 dried red chillies, or 1 fresh red chilli
- 5 teaspoons sugar
- juice and pulp of ¼ lime
- 4 tablespoons *nam pla* (fish sauce)
- 5 tablespoons water

1 Pound the garlic, chillies and sugar in a mortar using a pestle. Alternatively, place the ingredients in a bowl and mash them with the back of a spoon.

2 Stir in the lime juice and pulp, then the *nam pla* and water. Mix well to combine the ingredients. Use as required.

Makes about 150 ml (¼ pint)

Thai Prawn Toasts

These delicious toasts can be eaten on their own, but a few mooli and green pepper strips make an attractive accompaniment.

Mooli is from the same vegetable family as radish, with which it can be substituted, but it is much larger and has a slightly less peppery taste.

Preparation time: 20 minutes
Cooking time: 15–20 minutes

- 75 g (3 oz) uncooked prawns, peeled, deveined (see page 8) and minced
- 125 g (4 oz) minced pork
- 1 tablespoon finely chopped fresh coriander leaves, plus extra to garnish
- 1 tablespoon finely chopped spring onion
- 1 teaspoon Garlic Mixture (see page 9)
- 1 tablespoon *nam pla* (fish sauce)
- 1 egg, beaten
- 5 slices white bread
- 5 tablespoons sesame seeds
- vegetable oil for deep-frying

TO SERVE (OPTIONAL):
- plum sauce
- ¼ green pepper, very thinly sliced
- wide strips of raw mooli

1 Put the minced prawns and pork in a bowl with the coriander leaves, spring onion, Garlic Mixture and *nam pla*. Add the egg and mix well.

2 Cut each slice of bread into 4 pieces of roughly equal size. Spread each piece of bread with the pork and prawn mixture, using a knife to press the mixture firmly on to the bread. Sprinkle the sesame seeds on top.

3 Pour about 2.5 cm (1 inch) of oil into a wok and heat to 180–190°C (350–375°F) or until a cube of bread browns in *30 seconds*. Add the pieces of bread a few at a time, with the topping side facing downwards. Cook over a moderate heat for *6–8 minutes*, then turn over the bread and cook the other side until golden.

4 Remove with a slotted spoon, drain on kitchen paper, garnish wih coriander and serve hot with plum sauce, very thin slices of pepper and strips of mooli.

Serves 4

Fish and Seafood

Quick-cooking fish and seafood are ideal ingredients for stylish wok dishes and this chapter is full of recipes to inspire, from aromatic and economical Five-spice Fish to succulent Chilli Scallops. Creamy curries, rich with coconut milk, are balanced by light seafood stir-fries with crispy vegetables in dishes for all occasions.

Five Spice Fish

Serve this deliciously spiced mackerel with an oriental salad – a mixture of shredded water chestnuts, bamboo shoots and Chinese cabbage with bean sprouts and spring onions. Dress the salad with a few drops of sesame oil mixed with a crushed garlic clove, some sunflower or other light oil and a little lemon juice.

Preparation time: 15 minutes
Cooking time: 10–15 minutes

- 4 small mackerel, gutted
- 1 tablespoon plain flour
- ½ teaspoon five spice powder
- 2 tablespoons oil
- 1 celery stick, chopped
- pared rind of 1 small lemon, finely sliced

- 1 tablespoon soy sauce

GARNISH:

- a few spring onions, sliced
- lime wedges

TO SERVE:

- boiled rice
- mixed salad leaves

1 Cut off and discard the heads from the fish, then open out the fish and press them flat. Rinse the mackerel and dry them on kitchen paper.

2 To bone the mackerel – or any other round fish of this type, such as a herring – lay the fish flat on a board with the skin side uppermost. Press down firmly along the length of the back bone, then turn over the fish and lift off the bones which should be freed from the flesh. Remove any stray bones and the fish is ready for use.

3 Mix the flour with the five spice powder and sprinkle this over the flesh of the mackerel. Heat the oil in a wok and place the fish in the pan, arranging them so that they all fit neatly around the sides. Cook until brown and crisp underneath, turning them round once to ensure that they cook evenly. Then turn over the fish and cook the other side until brown and crisp.

4 Transfer the cooked fish on to 4 warm serving plates and add the celery and lemon rind to the fat remaining in the pan. Stir-fry quickly for *2 minutes*, then sprinkle in the soy sauce and top the fish with this mixture. Garnish with spring onions and lime wedges and serve immediately with boiled rice and a mixed salad.

Serves 4

variation
Five Spice Monkfish

1 Replace the mackerel with 500 g (1 lb) monkfish tail, skinned and cut into chunky pieces. Coat the pieces in the flour and five spice mixture as in the main recipe and fry in batches for *4–5 minutes* per batch, or until golden on all sides.

2 Serve immediately and garnish as in the main recipe.

Thai Yellow Prawn Curry

Preparation time: 10 minutes
Cooking time: 15 minutes

- 3 tablespoons groundnut oil
- 1 quantity Yellow Curry
  Paste (see page 10)
- 125 ml (4 fl oz) water
- 250 ml (8 fl oz) Coconut Milk
  (see page 9)
- 20 uncooked king prawns,
  peeled and deveined (see
  page 8)
- 2 teaspoons *nam pla* (fish
  sauce)

- 1 teaspoon lime juice
- salt and pepper
- boiled rice, to serve

GARNISH:

- 3 spring onions, sliced into
  strips
- 2 red chillies, finely sliced
- 1 tablespoon chopped fresh
  coriander

1 Heat the oil in a wok, add the curry paste and fry over gentle heat, stirring, for *4 minutes*, until the paste is fragrant. Stir the measured water into the curry paste, bring to the boil and cook over a high heat for *2 minutes* to reduce the paste.

2 Stir the Coconut Milk into the curry paste and then add the prawns. Cook the curry over a medium heat, stirring occasionally, for about *6 minutes* or until the prawns turn pink and are cooked through.

3 Stir in the *nam pla* and lime juice, and season to taste with salt and pepper. Transfer to a warm serving plate. Serve, garnished with the spring onion strips, chillies and coriander, and accompanied by boiled rice.

Serves 4

variation
Thai Yellow Squid Curry

1 Replace the prawns with 375 g (12 oz) squid rings. Add the squid to the Coconut Milk and curry paste in the wok and cook, stirring, for *5 minutes*.

2 Continue as in the main recipe and serve hot.

Stir-fried Squid with Mixed Vegetables

Do not overcook the squid or it will become tough and chewy.
When buying, remember that squid are at their most tender when small.

Preparation time: 20 minutes, plus marinating
Cooking time: 7–10 minutes

- 425 g (14 oz) squid
- 2 slices fresh root ginger, peeled and finely chopped
- 1 tablespoon rice wine or dry sherry
- 1 tablespoon cornflour
- 15 g (½ oz) dried shiitake mushrooms, soaked in hot water for *30 minutes*
- 4 tablespoons oil
- 2 spring onions, cut into 2.5 cm (1 inch) lengths
- 250 g (8 oz) broccoli or cauliflower, cut into florets
- 2 carrots, cut into diamond-shaped chunks
- 1 teaspoon salt
- 1 teaspoon sugar
- 1 teaspoon sesame oil
- noodles, to serve (optional)

1 First clean the squid. Cut off and discard the head and tentacles, then pull out and discard the transparent backbones and ink sacs. Cut the flesh into thin slices or rings. Place in a bowl with half the ginger, the wine and cornflour. Mix well, then leave to marinate for about *20 minutes*.

2 Meanwhile, drain the shiitake mushrooms and slice them into small pieces, discarding any tough stalks.

3 Heat 2 tablespoons of the oil in a wok and add the spring onions and remaining ginger, then add the broccoli or cauliflower, carrots and shiitake mushrooms. Add the salt and sugar and continue cooking until the vegetables are tender, adding a little water if necessary. Remove the vegetables from the wok with a slotted spoon. Discard any liquid from the wok.

4 Heat the remaining oil in the wok and stir-fry the squid for *1 minute*. Return the vegetables to the wok, add the sesame oil and mix together well. Serve hot with noodles, if liked.

Serves 4

King Prawn and Coconut Curry

Preparation time: 10 minutes
Cooking time: 15 minutes

- 2 tablespoons groundnut oil
- 1 teaspoon turmeric
- 150 ml (¼ pint) water
- 150 ml (¼ pint) Coconut Milk (see page 9)
- juice of 1 lime
- 2 teaspoons soft brown sugar
- 16 uncooked king prawns, peeled and deveined (see page 8)
- salt and pepper

SPICE PASTE:
- 2 red chillies, deseeded and chopped
- 2 shallots, chopped
- 1 lemon grass stalk, chopped
- 2.5 cm (1 inch) fresh root ginger, chopped
- ¼ teaspoon Thai shrimp paste

GARNISH:
- 4 spring onions, sliced into thin strips
- thin slices of coconut
- 1 tablespoon desiccated coconut

1 Place all the ingredients for the spice paste in a blender or spice mill and blend to produce a thick paste. Alternatively, pound the ingredients in a mortar with a pestle.

2 Heat the oil in a wok, add the paste and turmeric and then cook over a gentle heat, stirring frequently, for *3 minutes*.

3 Add the measured water to the pan, mix well and simmer gently for *3 minutes*. Stir in the Coconut Milk, lime juice, sugar and salt to taste. Simmer for a further *3 minutes*.

4 Add the prawns to the curry and cook for *4–5 minutes* until they turn pink and are cooked through. Season to taste.

5 Transfer the curry to a warm serving dish and serve immediately, garnished with spring onions, coconut slices and desiccated coconut.

Serves 4

Chilli Scallops

Preparation time: 10 minutes, plus marinating
Cooking time: 5 minutes

- 8 large scallops, with deep
  shells, if possible
- 2 tablespoons sunflower oil,
  plus extra for frying
- 1 teaspoon sesame oil
- 1 tablespoon dark soy sauce
- 1 teaspoon grated fresh root
  ginger
- pinch of five spice powder

- 1 tablespoon Thai Red Curry
  Paste (see page 10)
- 1 tablespoon chopped fresh
  coriander leaves
- 1–2 tablespoons sesame
  seeds
- 150 ml (¼ pint) Fish or
  Vegetable Stock (see page 9)
- coriander sprigs, to garnish

1 Thoroughly wash the scallop shells in hot soapy water, scrubbing off any dirt, then rinse and dry them. If the shells are unavailable, use small dishes instead.

2 Mix together the sunflower and sesame oils, soy sauce, ginger, five spice powder, Thai Red Curry Paste and chopped coriander in a shallow dish. Add the scallops, turn them to coat them well in the spice mixture and leave to marinate for at least *1 hour*.

3 Remove the scallops from their marinade and coat them with the sesame seeds. Scrape the marinade into a saucepan and pour in the stock. Bring to the boil, then simmer until reduced by half.

4 Heat a little oil in a wok. When very hot, add the scallops and fry for *1 minute* on each side. Serve the scallops either in their shells or in small dishes. Pour the reduced marinade over the scallops and serve garnished with coriander sprigs.

Serves 4

variation
Chilli Mackerel Steaks

1 Ask the fishmonger to fillet a large mackerel. Cut them in half and coat them in the spice mixture instead of the scallops. Continue as in the main recipe, then cook the mackerel pieces in the very hot wok for about 2 minutes on each side.

2 Serve hot on warm plates, drizzled with the marinade and garnished with coriander sprigs.

Crab Curry with Coconut

Stems of fresh lemon grass can be bought in oriental stores and some large supermarkets. They are frequently used in Thai cooking for their strong, aromatic citrus flavour. In this recipe, the whole stem is bruised to help release the flavour into the coconut sauce, and the stem is then removed before serving.

Preparation time: 15 minutes
Cooking time: 25 minutes

- 3 tablespoons vegetable oil
- 1 small onion, finely chopped
- 5 cm (2 inches) fresh root ginger, finely chopped
- 4 garlic cloves, crushed
- 2 teaspoons chilli powder, or to taste
- 2 teaspoons ground coriander
- 1 teaspoon turmeric
- dark and white meat from 1 large dressed crab
- 300 ml (½ pint) Coconut Milk (see page 9)
- 1 lemon grass stalk, bruised, or strip of pared lemon rind
- ½ teaspoon salt

GARNISH:

- 2 tablespoons finely chopped fresh coriander
- thin slices of coconut
- ½ red pepper, very finely sliced

1 Heat the oil in a wok until hot. Add the onion, ginger and garlic, and stir-fry for *2–3 minutes* until softened, taking care not to let the ingredients brown. Add the chilli powder, ground coriander and turmeric, and stir-fry for a further *1–2 minutes*.

2 Lightly mix in the dark crab meat, Coconut Milk, lemon grass and salt. Bring the mixture slowly to the boil, stirring constantly, then simmer for about *15 minutes* or until thickened, stirring frequently.

3 Turn the heat down to very low. Remove and discard the lemon grass or lemon rind. Add the white crab meat to the coconut sauce and heat through very gently, shaking the wok occasionally and taking care neither to break up the pieces of crab too much, nor to allow the sauce to burn on the bottom of the wok. Garnish with chopped coriander, slices of coconut and strips of red pepper. Serve at once.

Serves 2–3

Fish in Tamarind Sauce

Preparation time: 15 minutes
Cooking time: 20 minutes

- 1 John Dory or lemon sole, filleted
- oil for deep-frying

TAMARIND SAUCE:
- 3 tablespoons vegetable oil
- 2–3 garlic cloves, crushed
- 1–2 red or green chillies, deseeded and finely chopped, or to taste
- 125 ml (4 fl oz) Tamarind Water (see page 9)
- 1 tablespoon *nam pla* (fish sauce)

- 3 tablespoons soft brown sugar
- ½ head of white cabbage, shredded (optional), to serve

GARNISH:
- 2 tablespoons chopped fresh coriander leaves
- 1 red pepper, cored, deseeded and chopped
- 1 green pepper, cored, deseeded and chopped

1 Pat the fish dry with kitchen paper. Heat the oil for deep-frying in the wok to 180–190°C (350–375°F), or until a cube of bread browns in *30 seconds*. Deep-fry the fish fillets for *10–15 minutes* until golden brown. Using a slotted spoon, carefully remove the fish from the oil and drain it on kitchen paper. Transfer the fish to a serving dish and keep hot.

2 Meanwhile, make the Tamarind Sauce. Heat the vegetable oil in a small saucepan, add the garlic and chilli, and stir-fry for about *2 minutes* until golden, but not brown. Stir in the Tamarind Water, *nam pla* and brown sugar, and bring to the boil. Cook for a further *3 minutes*, stirring continuously.

3 Pour the sauce over the fish. Garnish with chopped coriander and chopped peppers. Serve at once, with a salad of shredded cabbage, if liked.

Serves 4

Prawns with Broccoli

Preparation time: 10 minutes, plus marinating
Cooking time: 5 minutes

- 250 g (8 oz) cooked king prawns, peeled and deveined (see page 8)
- 1 slice fresh root ginger, peeled and finely chopped
- 1 tablespoon medium or dry sherry
- 1 egg white
- 1 teaspoon cornflour
- 3 tablespoons vegetable oil
- 2 spring onions, finely chopped
- 250 g (8 oz) broccoli, cut into florets
- 1 teaspoon salt
- ½ teaspoon sugar

1 Wash the prawns, and dry them thoroughly on kitchen paper. Split each prawn in half lengthways and then cut it into small pieces.

2 Put the prawn pieces in a small bowl with the ginger, sherry, egg white and cornflour. Stir well and leave in a cool place or in the refrigerator to marinate for about *20 minutes*.

3 Heat 1 tablespoon of the oil in a wok and add the prawn mixture. Stir-fry over a moderate heat for about *30 seconds*. Remove from the wok with a slotted spoon.

4 Heat the remaining oil in the wok. Add the spring onions and broccoli and stir well. Add the salt and sugar, then stir-fry until the broccoli is just tender. Stir in the cooked prawns and serve hot.

Serves 2–3

Fish with Black Bean Sauce

Black bean sauce, which is rich and delicious, is a traditional accompaniment to fish and chicken in oriental dishes. Salted black beans are small wrinkled black beans with a pungent, salty taste. They are sold in oriental supermarkets or delicatessens in packets or they are sometimes described as fermented beans and sold in cans.

Preparation time: 15 minutes
Cooking time: 25–30 minutes

- sesame oil, for frying
- 25 g (1 oz) fresh root ginger, peeled and cut into fine strips
- 1 large garlic clove, chopped
- 3 tablespoons salted black beans
- 1 tablespoon lemon juice
- 2 tablespoons soy sauce
- 2 teaspoons sugar
- 150 ml (¼ pint) dry sherry

- 750 g (1½ lb) thick white fish fillet, in 2 pieces (for example, cod, haddock or coley), skinned
- 4 large spring onions, finely sliced diagonally, plus extra to garnish
- 1 red pepper, cored, deseeded, grilled and cut into fine strips, to garnish
- rice noodles, to serve (optional)

1 Heat a little sesame oil in a wok and add the ginger and garlic with the black beans. Stir-fry for *2 minutes*, then stir in the lemon juice, soy sauce, sugar and sherry.

2 Lay the fish fillets in the sauce in the wok. Simmer gently for *20–25 minutes*, by which time the fish should be cooked through. Sprinkle the spring onions over the top of the fish, cook for just a few minutes longer, then transfer the fish and sauce to a warm serving dish or alternatively, divide into 4 and serve on individual plates. Serve immediately with rice noodles, if liked, and garnished with the red pepper strips and spring onions.

Serves 4

variation

Chicken with Black Bean Sauce

1 Substitute 750 g (1½ lb) thinly sliced boneless, skinless chicken for the fish. Add to the sauce and simmer for 15–20 minutes, or until cooked through.

2 Continue as in the main recipe and serve hot.

Chicken, Pork and Beef

The versatility of the wok means it can be used in both western and oriental cooking. Chinese classics, like Crispy Wontons or Steamed Chicken Dumplings, are included in this chapter with exotic dishes, like Thai Green Chicken Curry. Alternatively, stir up a Hot Turkey Salad as a speedy supper or cook Oriental Duck with Pineapple to succulent perfection for a dinner party.

Ginger Chicken with Honey

This dish tastes even better if it is cooked a day in advance and then thoroughly reheated before being served.

Preparation time: 15 minutes, plus soaking
Cooking time: 10–15 minutes

- 50 g (2 oz) fresh root ginger, peeled and finely chopped
- 2 tablespoons vegetable oil
- 3 boneless, skinless chicken breasts, chopped
- 3 chicken livers, chopped
- 1 onion, finely sliced
- 3 garlic cloves, crushed
- 2 tablespoons dried black fungus (cloud's ears), soaked in hot water for *20 minutes*
- 2 tablespoons soy sauce
- 1 tablespoon honey
- 5 spring onions, chopped
- 1 red chilli, finely sliced into strips, to garnish
- rice sticks, to serve (optional)

1 Mix the ginger with a little cold water, then drain and squeeze it dry.

2 Heat the oil in a wok and add the chicken breasts and livers. Fry the chicken mixture over a moderate heat for *5 minutes*, then remove it with a slotted spoon and set aside.

3 Add the onion to the wok and fry it gently until soft, then add the garlic and the drained mushrooms and stir-fry for *1 minute*. Return the chicken mixture to the wok.

4 Stir together the soy sauce and honey in a bowl until blended, then pour this over the chicken and stir well. Add the drained ginger and stir-fry for *2–3 minutes*. Finally, add the spring onions. Serve at once, garnished with strips of red chilli and accompanied by rice sticks, if liked.

Serves 4

variation
Ginger Duck with Honey

1 Substitute 4 boneless duck breasts for the chicken. You can omit the chicken livers if you prefer.

2 Continue as in the main recipe, adding 1 head shredded bok choi or half a shredded Chinese cabbage *2–3 minutes* before serving.

Thai Green Chicken Curry

Preparation time: 10 minutes
Cooking time: 25 minutes

- 2 tablespoons groundnut oil
- 2.5 cm (1 inch) fresh root ginger, finely chopped
- 2 shallots, chopped
- 4 tablespoons Thai Green Curry Paste (see page 10)
- 625 g (1¼ lb) boneless, skinless chicken thighs, cut into 5 cm (2 inch) pieces
- 300 ml (½ pint) Coconut Milk (see page 9)
- 4 tablespoons *nam pla* (fish sauce)
- 1 teaspoon palm sugar or soft brown sugar
- 3 kaffir lime leaves, finely chopped
- 1 green chilli, deseeded and finely sliced
- salt and pepper
- fried chopped garlic, to garnish
- rice sticks, to serve (optional)

1 Heat the oil in a wok. Add the ginger and shallots and stir-fry over low heat for about *3 minutes* or until softened. Add the Thai Green Curry Paste and fry for *2 minutes*.

2 Add the chicken to the wok, stir until evenly coated in the spice mixture and fry for *3 minutes* to seal the chicken pieces. Stir in the Coconut Milk and bring the curry to the boil. Reduce the heat and cook the curry over a low heat, stirring occasionally, for about *10 minutes* or until the chicken is cooked through and the sauce has thickened.

3 Stir in the *nam pla*, palm sugar or soft brown sugar, kaffir lime leaves and chilli. Cook the curry for a further *5 minutes*, then add salt and pepper to taste. Garnish the curry with fried garlic and serve rice sticks as an accompaniment, if liked.

Serves 4

Thai Red Chicken Curry

Preparation time: 10 minutes
Cooking time: 25–30 minutes

- 2 tablespoons groundnut oil
- 1 small onion, finely chopped
- 1 lemon grass stalk, finely chopped
- 3 tablespoons Thai Red Curry Paste (see page 10)
- 625 g (1¼ lb) boneless, skinless chicken breasts
- 300 ml (½ pint) Coconut Milk (see page 9)
- 5 kaffir lime leaves, finely shredded
- 2 teaspoons soft brown sugar
- 1 tablespoon chopped Thai sweet basil leaves
- 1 tablespoon *nam pla* (fish sauce)
- 50 g (2 oz) salted peanuts, roughly chopped
- salt and pepper

GARNISH:

- handful Thai sweet basil
- lemon grass strips

1 Heat the groundnut oil in a wok. Add the onion, lemon grass and Thai Red Curry Paste. Cook over a gentle heat, stirring occasionally, for *3 minutes*.

2 Cut the chicken into bite-sized pieces and add to the wok. Stir to coat the chicken evenly in the paste and fry for a further *3 minutes*.

3 Stir in the Coconut Milk, kaffir lime leaves and soft brown sugar. Bring to the boil, then reduce the heat and cook the curry, stirring occasionally, for *15 minutes*, or until the chicken is cooked through.

4 Stir in the Thai sweet basil leaves, *nam pla* and peanuts, then cook the curry for a further *3 minutes*. Taste and adjust the seasoning, if necessary.

5 Serve freshly cooked, garnished with whole Thai sweet basil leaves and lemon grass strips, if liked.

Serves 4

Steamed Chicken Dumplings

Preparation time: 45 minutes
Cooking time: 20 minutes

- 500 g (1 lb) plain flour
- 300 ml (½ pint) water
- 1 small cabbage, separated into leaves
- Tangy Chilli Sauce (see page 25), to serve

FILLING:

- 500 g (1 lb) boneless, skinless chicken breasts
- 250 g (8 oz) can bamboo shoots, drained and chopped
- 3 spring onions, finely chopped
- 3 slices fresh root ginger, peeled and finely chopped
- 2 teaspoons sugar
- 2 teaspoons light soy sauce
- 2 tablespoons dry sherry
- 2 tablespoons Chicken Stock (see page 9)
- 1 teaspoon sesame oil
- salt

1 Sift the flour into a large mixing bowl and pour in the water. Mix thoroughly to form a stiff dough. Knead for *5 minutes* and then place the dough in a bowl, cover with a damp cloth and allow to stand for *10 minutes*.

2 Meanwhile, make the filling. Cut the chicken into small bite-size pieces and place in a bowl with the bamboo shoots, spring onions, ginger, a little salt, the sugar, soy sauce, sherry, stock and sesame oil. Thoroughly mix all the ingredients.

3 Cut the dough in half and form each piece into a long roll. Cut each roll into 16 slices and then flatten these into rounds. Roll out to circles, about 7.5 cm/3 inches in diameter. Place 1 tablespoon of filling in the centre of each circle of dough. Gather up the edges of the dough circles around the filling and twist them at the top to seal in the filling.

4 Line 1 large or 2 small bamboo steamers with the cabbage leaves. Place the dumplings on the leaves and steam, covered, over a wok of boiling water for *20 minutes*. Do not allow the wok to boil dry. Serve hot with Tangy Chilli Sauce.

Serves 8

Chicken, Aubergine and Bamboo Shoot Curry

Preparation time: 10 minutes
Cooking time: 25 minutes

- 3 tablespoons vegetable oil
- 2 tablespoons Thai Red
  Curry Paste (see page 10)
- 300 g (10 oz) boneless,
  skinless chicken breast,
  finely sliced
- 4 tablespoons *nam pla* (fish
  sauce)
- 3 kaffir lime leaves
- 600 ml (1 pint) water

- 3 small green aubergines,
  quartered
- 125 g (4 oz) canned bamboo
  shoots, finely sliced
- 2 green chillies, deseeded
  and finely sliced, plus extra
  to garnish
- handful of Thai sweet basil,
  to garnish
- boiled rice, to serve

1 Heat the oil in a wok over a moderate heat. Add the Thai
Red Curry Paste and stir-fry for *1 minute*. Add the chicken,
nam pla and kaffir lime leaves, and stir-fry for *5 minutes*.

2 Pour in the measured water and bring the curry to the boil,
then lower the heat before adding the aubergines and
bamboo shoots. Stir well and simmer for *10 minutes*, stirring
occasionally. Stir in the green chillies.

3 Garnish the curry with Thai sweet basil and green chilli
slices, then serve it with boiled rice, if liked.

Serves 4

Hot Turkey Salad

This is a delicious dish in which lemon grass is used to give simple stir-fried turkey a wonderful flavour and aroma. Serve this hot salad with a rice dish, new potatoes or a baked potato.

Preparation time: 15 minutes
Cooking time: 10 minutes

- 3 thick lemon grass stalks
- 25 g (1 oz) fresh root ginger, sliced
- 50 g (2 oz) butter
- 1 garlic clove
- 750 g (1½ lb) boneless, skinless turkey breast, cut into bite-sized cubes
- 1 tablespoon dark soy sauce
- 1 head curly endive
- 3 spring onions, chopped
- 1 lemon, cut into wedges, to garnish

1 Cut the lemon grass in half lengthways and then cut the strips in half widthways and mix them with the ginger.

2 Melt the butter in a wok, crush the garlic into it and add the lemon grass and ginger. Cook, stirring continuously, for *2 minutes*, then add the turkey and continue stir-frying until the meat has browned all over and is cooked through. Add the soy sauce and cook gently for a few minutes more.

3 Arrange the endive leaves on a serving dish. Sprinkle the spring onions over the endive. Arrange the turkey on top and pour over any juices from the wok. Serve immediately, garnished with the lemon wedges. When served, the juice can be squeezed from these to add a little extra bite.

Serves 4

variation
Warm Duck Salad

1 Add the lemon grass, ginger, butter and garlic to the wok as in the main recipe, then substitute 750 g (1½ lb) thinly sliced duck breasts for the turkey.

2 Stir-fry and continue as in the main recipe. Serve on a bed of baby rocket and spinach leaves instead of endive leaves. Garnish with coriander leaves.

Oriental Duck with Pineapple

The combination of simmering and frying makes the duck meat in this dish both tender and well flavoured. You can use canned pineapple in natural juice instead of the fresh fruit, but the end result warrants buying a fresh pineapple. Serve with steamed or boiled rice to make a complete meal.

Preparation time: 20 minutes
Cooking time: 1 hour 10 minutes

- 1 oven-ready duck
- 1.2 litres (2 pints) water
- 3 tablespoons dark soy
  sauce
- 1 fresh pineapple
- sesame oil
- 2 green chillies, deseeded
  and thinly sliced

- 1 large garlic clove
- 250 g (8 oz) can water
  chestnuts, drained and
  sliced
- 1 bunch spring onions, sliced
  diagonally

1 Cut the duck in half lengthways, using a meat cleaver and poultry scissors. Place the halves in a wok and pour in the measured water, then add 1 tablespoon of the soy sauce. Put the lid on the wok and bring to the boil. Reduce the heat so that the liquid simmers steadily and cook for *1 hour*.

2 While the duck is cooking, prepare the pineapple: trim the leaves off the top and cut off the stalk end. Cut off the peel and cut out all the spines, then slice the fruit in half lengthways and remove the hard core. Cut the pineapple halves into slices and set them aside.

3 Remove the duck from its stock and set aside. Pour the stock out of the wok (this should be chilled and the fat skimmed off, then the stock can be used in oriental soups and stews) and wipe out the pan. Oil the wok with a little sesame oil.

4 When the duck is cool enough to handle, cut all the meat off the bones and slice it into pieces. Heat the wok and add the chillies. Crush the garlic into the wok and add the duck. Stir-fry until lightly browned, then add the water chestnuts and pineapple and cook for *1–2 minutes*. Stir in the remaining soy sauce and any juice from the fruit, and sprinkle with the spring onions. Cook for *1 minute* and serve immediately.

Serves 4

variation
Pineapple Duck Breasts

1 Use 4 boneless duck breasts instead of the whole bird. Add to the wok as in the main recipe.

2 When the duck is cooked, drain the stock and slice the duck across the grain. Continue as in the main recipe.

Thai Pork Curry

Preparation time: 20 minutes
Cooking time: 30 minutes

- 2 tablespoons groundnut oil
- 2 shallots, finely sliced
- 1 green chilli, deseeded and sliced
- 500 g (1 lb) pork fillet, sliced
- 1 tablespoon *nam pla* (fish sauce)
- ½ teaspoon soft brown sugar
- 150 ml (¼ pint) Coconut Milk (see page 9)
- 75 g (3 oz) drained canned bamboo shoots, plus extra to serve
- 2 tablespoons chopped fresh coriander

CURRY PASTE:
- 2 large dried red chillies, deseeded and chopped
- 3 garlic cloves, crushed
- 2 kaffir lime leaves, finely chopped
- 6 black peppercorns, crushed
- 1 tablespoon chopped lemon grass
- ½ teaspoon Thai shrimp paste

GARNISH:
- 1 red chilli, sliced into rings
- coriander sprigs

1 Blend all the curry paste ingredients to a thick paste in a blender or food processor. Alternatively, pound them to a paste in a mortar using a pestle.

2 Heat the oil in a wok. Add the shallots and chilli, and fry over a gentle heat, stirring, for *3 minutes*. Stir in the curry paste and fry for a further *1 minute*.

3 Stir in the pork, coating the pieces evenly in the spice mixture, then stir in the *nam pla* and brown sugar. Cook, stirring, for *3 minutes*. Pour in the Coconut Milk and bring the curry to the boil. Reduce the heat and simmer gently for *20 minutes*, stirring occasionally, until the pork is tender.

4 Stir in the bamboo shoots and chopped coriander. Cook for a final *2 minutes*, to heat through.

5 Garnish the curry with red chilli slices and coriander sprigs, and serve immediately with more bamboo shoots.

Serves 4

Fresh Ingredients

Specialist stores offer a bewildering range of exotic foods, but wide-ranging shopping trips are not necessary as most supermarkets are well stocked with a good selection of interesting and useful international ingredients.

Dried bean curd

Galangal

Fresh root ginger

Kaffir limes

Wonton wrappers

Bean curd

Wonton wrappers are small thin squares of yellow dough, which are used to make wontons, or dumplings. They freeze well and should be packed in small numbers to avoid thawing a large batch. **Galangal** or greater galangal, is a spice of the ginger family, with a slightly lighter flavour. **Fresh root ginger** is plump and juicy at its best. Avoid thick-skinned, shrivelled roots. Fresh ginger freezes very well in cling film or a small freezer bag. **Kaffir limes** are rough-skinned citrus fruit with a strong flavour. The rind, juice and leaves are all used. **Bean curd**, also known as tofu, is sold fresh in Oriental stores or vacuum-packed in supermarkets. It is highly nutritious, with a smooth texture and a bland flavour. **Dried bean curd** is used as a meat substitute in vegetarian dishes. It must be soaked before use, according to manufacturer's instructions. **Bean sprouts** are sprouted mung beans. Fresh are best as canned are not as crunchy. Cook quickly in order to preserve their texture.

Chillies

Lemon grass

Bean sprouts

Coriander

Green aubergines

Thai basil

Chinese cabbage

Pea aubergines

Green aubergines are small and round, with skin that ranges in colour from creamy white to pale green.

Chillies come in many shapes and sizes. The small slim varieties are often very hot. Avoid any form of contact between chillies and eyes or damaged skin, as their juices can cause severe irritation. Wash your hands thoroughly after preparing them.

Thai basil is also known as holy basil, as Hindus consider it to be a sacred herb. It is similar to sweet basil but with a spicy flavour. If Thai basil is not available, use sweet basil and add just a little finely chopped chilli.

Pea aubergines are tiny aubergines sold on the stalk, from which they should be picked for cooking.

Lemon grass is often used in Thai cooking and has a strong lemon flavour.

Coriander, also known as Chinese parsley, looks like flat-leaf parsley, but it has a distinctive, spicy flavour. The leaves, roots and seeds are all used in cooking. It is particularly popular in Chinese, Thai and other Oriental styles of cookery.

Chinese cabbage has a clean, delicate flavour and can be used raw or lightly cooked.

Pork Wontons

Wontons are a type of Chinese dumpling made from a dough similar to pasta. You can make your own wonton wrappers, as shown below, or you can buy them ready-prepared. Wontons can be either simmered in liquid or deep-fried to give crisp, light results. They are delicious served with steamed rice.

Preparation time: 45 minutes
Cooking time: 15–20 minutes

- 1 egg, beaten
- 1.2 litres (2 pints) Chicken Stock (see page 9)
- 2 carrots, peeled and cut into fine strips
- 250 g (8 oz) can bamboo shoots, drained and cut into fine strips
- 4 tablespoons dry sherry
- 1 small Chinese cabbage, sliced
- coriander sprigs, to garnish

WONTON WRAPPERS:
- 50 g (2 oz) plain flour
- 50 g (2 oz) cornflour
- 2 teaspoons baking powder
- pinch of salt
- 1 egg, lightly beaten
- 2 tablespoons water

FILLING:
- 125 g (4 oz) lean minced pork
- 2 tablespoons dried shrimps
- few drops of sesame oil
- 2 teaspoons soy sauce
- ½ small onion, very finely chopped

1 First make the wrappers. Sift the flours, baking powder and salt into a mixing bowl and make a well in the centre. Add the egg and water and mix to make a stiff dough. Turn out on to a lightly floured surface and knead thoroughly until very smooth. Work quickly so that the dough does not stick to the work surface and try to avoid using lots of flour. Divide the dough in half and keep the 2 portions covered with clingfilm while you prepare the filling.

2 Mix the pork with the shrimps, a few drops of sesame oil, the soy sauce and onion. Stir well to combine the ingredients.

3 Take one portion of dough (keep the other covered) and roll it out on a well-floured surface until it is very thin. It should form a square of about 25 cm (10 inches). The thinner the

dough becomes, the better the results, but take care not to rip it as it is very difficult to patch up any holes. Trim the edges and cut out 9 small squares. Roll out each of these until very thin and about 10 cm (4 inches) square.

4 Place a little filling (less than a teaspoonful) in the middle of each piece of dough and brush the edges with a little beaten egg. Gather up the dough to enclose the filling completely, sealing it in well but leaving the edges of the dough free. The filled wontons should look like small gathered muslin herb bags. Place the filled wontons on a large floured board or plate. Repeat with the second portion of dough.

5 Pour the stock into a wok and bring it to the boil, then reduce the heat so that it simmers very gently. Cook the wontons in the stock, a few at a time, for *5 minutes*. Do not allow the stock to boil too rapidly or the wontons may break up and loose their filling. Remove the cooked wontons from the stock with a slotted spoon and set aside.

6 When all the wontons are cooked, bring the stock to a rapid boil in the open wok and boil hard until it has reduced by half. Add the carrot and bamboo shoot strips to the stock with the sherry, and boil for *1 minute*. Add the cabbage and reduce the heat, then return the wontons to the wok and simmer for *2 minutes* to heat through. Serve immediately, garnished with coriander sprigs.

Serves 4

variations

Chicken Wontons

1 Prepare the wontons by the same technique used in the main recipe, but using 2 small boneless, skinless chicken breasts instead of the pork filling. Cut the chicken into 18 small pieces and toss them in a pinch of Chinese five spice powder, 1 crushed garlic clove and 2 tablespoons soy sauce. Allow the chicken to marinate for about *30 minutes* before using the pieces to fill the wontons as in the main recipe.

2 Cook and serve the wontons either as in the main recipe or as in the following variation.

Crispy Wontons

1 Prepare the wontons as in the main recipe.

2 Heat oil for deep-frying to 180–190°C (350–375°F), or until a cube of bread browns in *30 seconds*, and deep-fry the wontons in batches until they are puffed, crisp and golden.

3 Drain the wontons on kitchen paper and serve at once. They may be served as a starter, with a simple dipping sauce of soy sauce flavoured with sliced garlic or sliced chilli. Alternatively, serve with sweet and sour sauce and boiled rice.

Stuffed Thai Omelette

Preparation time: 10 minutes
Cooking time: 12–17 minutes

- 3 tablespoons vegetable oil
- 1 garlic clove, crushed
- 125 g (4 oz) minced pork
- 1 tablespoon *nam pla* (fish sauce)
- ½ teaspoon sugar
- 125 g (4 oz) finely chopped onion
- 1 tomato, skinned and chopped
- 3 eggs, beaten
- pepper

GARNISH:

- fresh coriander sprigs
- 2 red chillies, sliced stem to tip and opened out to look like flowers

1 Heat 2 tablespoons of the oil in a wok. Add the garlic and stir-fry quickly until just golden. Add the minced pork, *nam pla*, sugar, onion and tomato, and season with pepper.

2 Stir-fry the pork and vegetable mixture for *5–10 minutes*, until the pork is lightly browned and the onion is golden but not brown.

3 Heat the remaining oil in a clean wok, tilting it so that the oil coats the entire surface. Pour away and discard any excess oil. Add the beaten eggs, tilting the wok to form an omelette.

4 Put the stir-fried vegetable and pork mixture in the centre of the cooked omelette. Fold down the four sides like a parcel. Serve immediately, folded side down, garnished with coriander sprigs and chilli flowers.

Serves 2

Pork with Chilli and Basil

Preparation time: 10 minutes
Cooking time: 8–10 minutes

- 2 tablespoons vegetable oil
- 1 garlic clove, crushed
- 2 chillies, finely chopped, or to taste
- 125 g (4 oz) pork fillet, finely sliced
- ¼ teaspoon pepper
- 1 tablespoon *nam pla* (fish sauce)
- ½ teaspoon sugar
- 50 g (2 oz) canned bamboo shoots, very finely sliced (optional)
- 2 tablespoons finely chopped onion
- 2 tablespoons finely sliced red pepper
- 4 tablespoons Chicken or Vegetable Stock (see page 9)
- 2 handfuls of basil, plus extra to garnish
- 3–4 large red chillies, sliced, to garnish
- boiled rice, to serve

1 Heat the oil in a wok. Add the garlic and chillies and stir-fry until the garlic is just golden. Add the pork, pepper, *nam pla* and sugar, stirring constantly.

2 Stir in the bamboo shoots, if using, with the onion, red pepper and stock. Cook for *5 minutes*. Stir in the basil leaves and cook for *1 minute* more. Garnish with basil leaves and large slices of red chilli. Serve immediately with boiled rice.

Serves 4

variation
Steak with Chilli and Basil

Stir-fry the garlic and chillies as in the main recipe, then substitute 125 g (4 oz) rump steak instead of the pork. Continue as in the main recipe.

Mangetout and Beef Stir-fry

Preparation time: 15 minutes, plus marinating
Cooking time: about 8 minutes

- 250 g (8 oz) rump steak, finely sliced
- 2 tablespoons oyster sauce
- 1 tablespoon rice wine or dry sherry
- 1 teaspoon cornflour
- 4 tablespoons oil
- 2 spring onions, cut into 2.5 cm (1 inch) lengths
- 1 slice fresh root ginger, peeled and cut into strips
- 250 g (8 oz) mangetout, trimmed
- 1 teaspoon sugar
- salt

1 Cut the beef slices into narrow strips and put in a bowl with the oyster sauce, wine or sherry and cornflour. Mix well, then leave to marinate for about *20 minutes*.

2 Heat 2 tablespoons of the oil in a wok and stir-fry the spring onions and ginger for a few seconds. Add the beef and stir-fry until evenly browned. Transfer the mixture to a warm serving dish and keep hot.

3 Heat the remaining oil in the wok and stir-fry the mangetout, sugar and salt to taste for about *2 minutes*. Do not allow the mangetout to overcook, or they will lose their texture and colour. Add the mangetout to the beef and mix well. Serve immediately.

Serves 4

variation
Stir-fried Sugar Snaps with Baby Corn and Beef

1 Prepare and cook the beef as in the main recipe.

2 Substitute 125 g (4 oz) baby corn on the cob and 125 g (4 oz) sugar snaps for the mangetout. Cook for 2–3 minutes, mixing well.

3 Serve hot with steamed rice and garnished with some fine red pepper strips.

Beef with Ginger and Jelly Mushrooms

Preparation time: 10 minutes, plus soaking
Cooking time: 10 minutes

- 125 g (4 oz) dried jelly mushrooms, black fungus (cloud's ears) or shiitake mushrooms
- 2 tablespoons vegetable oil
- 1 garlic clove, crushed
- 125 g (4 oz) rump steak, finely sliced
- 2 tablespoons finely chopped fresh root ginger
- 1 tablespoon black bean sauce
- ¼ teaspoon pepper
- 1 teaspoon sugar
- 4 spring onions, chopped
- 125 ml (4 fl oz) Chicken Stock (see page 9)
- 2 spring onions, sliced into strips, to garnish
- boiled rice, to serve (optional)

1 Soak the mushrooms in boiling water for *20 minutes*. Drain, squeezing out excess liquid, remove any tough stems and slice the caps.

2 Heat the oil in a wok. Add the garlic and stir-fry until golden. Add the steak, ginger, black bean sauce, pepper and sugar. Cook, stirring constantly, until the steak is lightly browned. Stir in the mushrooms, spring onions and Chicken Stock, and cook for *5 minutes*.

3 Garnish with strips of spring onion and serve immediately with boiled rice.

Serves 4

Hot Thai Beef Salad

This contrast of fiery hot meat and refreshing, colourful fruit looks great and tastes wonderful. Thai food is usually hot and chillies are a favourite ingredient, but if you prefer a milder taste, include only a few of the chilli seeds, or even none at all.

Preparation time: 15 minutes
Cooking time: 5–10 minutes

- 2 tablespoons vegetable oil
- 500 g (1 lb) rump or fillet steak, cut across the grain into thin strips
- 3 garlic cloves, finely chopped
- 2 green chillies, finely sliced into rings
- juice of 2 lemons
- 1 tablespoon *nam pla* (fish sauce)
- 2 teaspoons caster sugar
- 2 ripe papayas, peeled and finely sliced
- ½ large cucumber, cut into matchstick strips
- 75 g (3 oz) bean sprouts
- 1 head crisp lettuce, shredded
- chilli sauce, to serve (optional)

1 Heat a wok, add the oil and place over a moderate heat until hot. Add the steak, garlic and chillies, increase the heat to high and stir-fry for *3–4 minutes* or until the steak is browned on all sides. Pour in the lemon juice and *nam pla*, add the sugar and stir-fry until sizzling.

2 Remove the wok from the heat. Remove the steak from the liquid with a slotted spoon and toss together with the papaya, cucumber, bean sprouts and lettuce. Drizzle the liquid from the wok over the salad ingredients as a dressing and serve hot with a bowl of chilli sauce, if liked.

Serves 4

variation

Thai Beef Salad with Mango

1 Cook the ingredients as in the main recipe, substituting 2 ripe mangoes for the papaya.

2 Serve hot on a bed of coriander instead of lettuce, and drizzled with the liquid from the wok.

Rice and Noodles

There is a fabulous range of flavours and textures in oriental rice and noodle dishes. Choose from piquant Thai Fried Rice, Creamy Rice with Fish and the simple but delicious Noodles with Cucumber. The following recipes offer an excellent opportunity for making the most of your wok.

Thai Fried Rice

The combination of chicken or meat and prawns is very tasty, and is extremely popular in the Far East.

Preparation time: 15 minutes
Cooking time: 25 minutes

- 250 g (8 oz) long-grain rice
- 750 ml (1¼ pints) water
- 1 small onion, chopped
- 1 garlic clove, finely sliced
- 3 dried red chillies, finely sliced
- 1 small bunch of fresh coriander, finely chopped, plus extra to garnish
- juice of 1 lime
- 2 tablespoons *nam pla* (fish sauce)

- 2 tablespoons vegetable oil
- 250 g (8 oz) boneless, skinless, cooked chicken, pork or beef, finely sliced
- 125 g (4 oz) peeled cooked prawns
- 1 teaspoon caster sugar, or to taste
- salt

GARNISH:
- 1 red chilli, finely sliced
- 2 spring onions, finely sliced

1 Rinse the rice in a sieve under cold running water and drain well. Then place it in a saucepan with the measured water and salt to taste. Bring to the boil, stir once, cover and simmer for *15–20 minutes*, or until the water has been absorbed by the rice. Turn the rice into a sieve and rinse it under cold running water. Set aside to drain well.

2 Meanwhile, purée the onion, garlic, chillies, coriander, lime juice and *nam pla* to a paste in a blender or food processor. Alternatively, pound the ingredients in a mortar with a pestle.

3 Heat a wok, add the oil and heat over a moderate heat until hot. Add the onion paste and stir-fry for *2–3 minutes*, then add the cooked rice, increase the heat to high and toss well to separate the grains.

4 Add the meat and prawns, then sprinkle in the sugar and stir-fry for *1–2 minutes* or until all the ingredients are combined and piping hot. Taste and add more salt or sugar if necessary. Serve hot, garnished with coriander, slices of red chilli and spring onion.

Serves 4

Pineapple Fried Rice

This simple, tasty dish may be topped with chopped roasted peanuts, if liked, before serving.

Preparation time: 10 minutes
Cooking time: 15–20 minutes

- 250 g (8 oz) long-grain rice
- 750 ml (1¼ pints) water
- 4 tablespoons vegetable oil
- 1 garlic clove, crushed
- 125 g (4 oz) ham, cubed
- 1 carrot, diced
- 4 tablespoons raisins
- ¼ green pepper, cored, deseeded and diced
- ¼ red pepper, cored, deseeded and diced
- 4 tablespoons *nam pla* (fish sauce)
- 1 tablespoon sugar
- 4 pineapple rings, diced
- salt and pepper
- 2 tablespoons chopped fresh coriander, to garnish

1 Rinse the rice in a sieve under cold running water and drain well. Then place the rice in a saucepan with the measured water and salt to taste. Bring to the boil, stir once, cover and simmer for *15–20 minutes* or until the water has been absorbed by the rice. Turn the rice into a sieve and rinse it under cold running water. Set aside the rice to drain.

2 Heat the oil in a wok. Add the garlic and stir-fry until just golden. Add the ham, carrot, raisins, green and red peppers, *nam pla* and sugar. Stir-fry for *5 minutes*.

3 Add the rice and pineapple, and season the mixture with pepper. Cook, stirring constantly, for a further *5 minutes*.

4 Serve immediately, garnished with chopped coriander.

Serves 4

Ten-variety Fried Rice

Preparation time: 25 minutes
Cooking time: 35 minutes

- 175 g (6 oz) long-grain rice
- 600 ml (1 pint) water
- 3½ tablespoons vegetable oil
- 1 egg, beaten
- 175 g (6 oz) skinless, boneless chicken breast, finely sliced
- 125–175 g (4–6 oz) pork fillet, finely sliced
- 1 red pepper, cored, deseeded and finely chopped
- 4 spring onions, finely sliced
- 2 garlic cloves, crushed
- 3 green chillies, deseeded and finely chopped

- 3 tomatoes, chopped
- 125 g (4 oz) peeled cooked prawns
- 125 g (4 oz) white crab meat, flaked
- salt
- cucumber strips, to garnish

SAUCE:

- 150 ml (¼ pint) Fish Stock (see page 9)
- 2 tablespoons soy sauce
- 1 tablespoon caster sugar
- 2 teaspoons lemon juice
- 2 teaspoons *nam pla* (fish sauce)

1 Rinse the rice in a sieve under cold running water and drain well. Then place the rice in a saucepan. Add the measured water and salt to taste and bring to the boil. Stir once, cover and simmer for *15–20 minutes*, or until the water is absorbed by the rice. Turn the rice into a sieve and rinse under cold running water. Set aside to drain.

2 Meanwhile, make an omelette. Heat 1 tablespoon of the oil in a wok and, when hot, add the beaten egg. Swirl the egg around the wok to form a thick skin. When cooked through, remove the omelette from the wok, allow it to cool, then roll it up tightly and slice it finely. Set the sliced omelette aside.

3 Mix the sauce ingredients together in a bowl and set aside.

4 Heat a wok, add another 1 tablespoon of oil and heat until hot. Add the chicken and pork, increase the heat to high and stir-fry for *3–4 minutes* or until lightly browned. Remove the wok from the heat, tip the contents into a bowl and set aside.

5 Add the remaining oil to the wok and heat until hot. Add the red pepper, spring onions, garlic and chillies and stir-fry for *2–3 minutes* or until softened. Add the tomatoes and cooked rice to the wok and stir well to mix. Return the chicken, pork and their juices to the wok and increase the heat to high. Pour in the sauce and toss the ingredients until they are combined, piping hot, and the grains of rice have separated.

6 Gently fold in the prawns and crab meat, taking care not to break up the crab too much. Heat through, shaking the wok occasionally, and season to taste. Serve topped with thin slices of omelette and garnished with cucumber strips.

Serves 3–4

Creamy Rice with Fish

Preparation time: 10 minutes
Cooking time: 30 minutes

- 175 g (6 oz) long-grain rice
- 1.6 litres (2¾ pints), plus
  2 tablespoons, Chicken
  Stock (see page 9)
- 3 tablespoons vegetable oil
- 1 tablespoon finely chopped
  garlic
- 500 g (1 lb) cod fillet, thinly
  sliced

- 2 tablespoons *nam pla* (fish
  sauce)
- 1 teaspoon pepper

GARNISH:

- 2 spring onions, shredded
- 2 celery sticks, very finely
  chopped

1 Rinse the rice several times in a sieve under running water, then drain well.

2 Bring 600 ml (1 pint) of the Chicken Stock to the boil in a large saucepan. Add the rice, then cook for *15–20 minutes* over a low heat, stirring from time to time. The rice should absorb most of the stock. Add the remaining 1 litre (1¾ pints) of Chicken Stock, bring back to the boil, then remove the pan from the heat.

3 Heat the oil in a wok, add the garlic and stir-fry until just golden. With a slotted spoon, remove the garlic and set aside.

4 Add the cod to the oil remaining in the wok and stir-fry for *4–6 minutes*, adding the remaining 2 tablespoons of stock, if necessary, to prevent the fish sticking to the wok.

5 As soon as the cod is cooked, add it to the rice together with the *nam pla* and pepper. Mix well and transfer to a serving dish.

6 Garnish the rice mixture with spring onion shreds, chopped celery and the reserved fried garlic. Serve immediately.

Serves 4

Storecupboard Ingredients

The right seasonings or accompaniments can transform familiar foods into Oriental specialities. Here are a few examples of excellent storecupboard ingredients. Store them in airtight containers and observe the manufacturer's recommended shelf life.

Tamarind paste

Galangal powder

Black beans

Dried shiitake mushrooms

Fermented black beans

Nam pla

Black beans are small, jet-black soya beans. They are available either dried or cooked and canned, and have a pleasantly distinctive earthy flavour.
Fermented black beans have a rich, salty flavour. They are moist and wrinkled, and

are often sold ground to a paste and mixed with spices to make black bean sauce.
Tamarind paste is made from the bitter tamarind pods of a large evergreen tree that grows in India. The inner sticky pulp is made into tamarind paste, which is sold

in dark brown-black blocks. It has an unusual flavour – at the same time tart and sweet. Dissolve it in water to make tamarind water.
Nam pla is a salty, highly flavoured sauce made from fermented salted fish, and is widely used as a seasoning or

condiment in South-east Asian cooking.
Dried shiitake mushrooms are widely used in Chinese cooking and other Oriental cuisines. They have a strong, distinctly musty flavour.
Galangal powder, also known as laos or dried

Palm sugar

Bean thread noodles

Shrimp paste

Wheat noodles

Black fungus

Rice sticks

Egg noodles

Rice paper spring roll wrappers

galangal, is a spice of the ginger family and has a similar flavour to ginger.

Black fungus, also known as cloud ear or dried wood ear, is a large, curly fungus which should be soaked, rinsed and shredded or cut up for use.

Palm sugar, or rock sugar, is extracted from palms.

Shrimp paste is made from fermented shrimps or prawns. It is very strong in both smell and flavour.

Egg noodles are used to make chow mein. There are many types, either fresh or dried, which are available in bundles or blocks.

Rice paper spring roll wrappers are available dried and become moist and flexible when they are brushed with egg or egg white.

Bean thread noodles also known as transparent or cellophane noodles are fine, clear noodles made from mung bean flour.

Wheat noodles, often used in soup, are available both fresh and dried.

Rice sticks are available in many forms. They are white and translucent, requiring brief cooking or soaking.

Noodles with Cucumber

Stir-fried cucumber tastes very good, particularly with garlic-flavoured noodles. Serve these noodles with meat or fish dishes. Extra ingredients can also be added to make this a main dish and suggestions for these are given below.

Preparation time: 15 minutes
Cooking time: 7–10 minutes

- 375 g (12 oz) egg noodles
- 1.2 litres (2 pints) boiling water
- pinch of salt
- ½ cucumber, peeled
- 2 tablespoons vegetable oil
- 2 green chillies, deseeded and finely sliced
- 1 red chilli, deseeded and finely sliced
- 1 bunch of spring onions, shredded
- 1 garlic clove

1 Place the noodles in the wok and pour the boiling water over them. Add a pinch of salt and bring to the boil, then put the lid on the wok and reduce the heat so that the water simmers rapidly. Cook for *3–5 minutes*, or according to packet instructions. Check to see if the noodles are cooked after *3 minutes* – they should be tender but not sticky.

2 While the noodles are cooking, cut the cucumber into matchstick strips.

3 Drain the noodles and heat the oil in the wok. Add the cucumber, red and green chillies and spring onions and cook, stirring, for *1 minute*. Crush the garlic into the wok and stir for *1 minute* more, then add the cooked noodles. Toss well to combine the ingredients and put the lid on the wok. Cook over gentle heat for about *2–3 minutes*, or until the noodles are hot. Serve immediately.

Serves 4

variations

This simple accompaniment can be turned into an interesting main dish by adding any of the following ingredients:

Noodles with Prawns and Ham

Preparation time: 15 minutes
Cooking time: 7–10 minutes

Add 250 g (8 oz) peeled cooked prawns and 250 g (8 oz) shredded cooked ham to the noodles when they are returned to the wok for reheating.

Spicy Chicken with Noodles

Preparation time: 20 minutes
Cooking time: 12–15 minutes

Cook 500 g (1 lb) shredded chicken breast and 25 g (1 oz) grated fresh root ginger in the oil in the wok for *5 minutes*, until lightly browned, before adding the cucumber and other vegetables.

Noodles with Pork and Water Chestnuts

Preparation time: 20 minutes
Cooking time: 15–18 minutes

Finely shred 250 g (8 oz) lean pork and fry this in the oil in the wok for *5–7 minutes*, or until lightly browned, before adding the cucumber and other vegetables. Add 250 g (8 oz) canned water chestnuts, drained and sliced, with the cucumber. If you like, sprinkle a few roasted sesame seeds over before serving.

Thai Noodles with Prawns

Nam pla is the Thai name for bottled fish sauce made from salted fish. It is an essential ingredient in Thai cooking and can be bought in oriental stores specializing in South-east Asian food. *Nam pla* is a useful storecupboard ingredient as it keeps indefinitely and can be added to all sorts of savoury foods to give them an oriental flavour. As an alternative in an emergency, try using a little anchovy essence and a drop or two of vinegar.

Preparation time: 10 minutes
Cooking time: 10 minutes

- 250 g (8 oz) rice sticks
- 2 tablespoons vegetable oil
- 125 g (4 oz) radishes, trimmed and thinly sliced
- 375 g (12 oz) uncooked tiger prawns, peeled and deveined (see page 8)
- juice of 1 lemon
- 1 tablespoon caster sugar
- 2 teaspoons *nam pla* (fish sauce)
- 1 teaspoon hot chilli powder, or to taste
- salt

GARNISH:

- Thai sweet basil sprigs
- 1 tablespoon chopped coriander

1 First cook the rice sticks in boiling salted water according to the packet instructions.

2 Meanwhile, heat the oil in a wok. Add the radishes, increase the heat to high and stir-fry for *30 seconds*. Add the prawns and stir-fry for *1–2 minutes* or until they turn pink. Add the lemon juice, sugar, *nam pla* and chilli powder and stir-fry for a further *1–2 minutes*.

3 Drain the rice sticks, add them to the prawn mixture and toss until evenly mixed. Serve immediately, garnished with basil sprigs and chopped coriander.

Serves 2–3

Fried Rice Sticks with Meat and Vegetables

This is a very adaptable dish, in which almost any tender cut of meat may be used, along with prawns or crab meat, if liked. The vegetables are equally interchangeable, as are the noodles. The important point is to remember to adjust the cooking times to suit the ingredients used.

Preparation time: 10 minutes
Cooking time: about 15 minutes

- 125 g (4 oz) rice sticks
- 125 g (4 oz) either boneless, skinless chicken breast, fillet steak, pork fillet, crab meat, uncooked prawns, peeled and deveined (see page 8), or a combination of these
- 2 tablespoons vegetable oil
- 1 garlic clove, crushed
- ½ teaspoon pepper
- 125 g (4 oz) vegetables, such as cauliflower florets, finely sliced courgettes or whole green beans
- 2 tablespoons dark soy sauce
- 2 tablespoons *nam pla* (fish sauce)
- 2 tablespoons sugar
- 1 egg, beaten
- omelette slices, to garnish (see page 70)

1 Cook the rice sticks in boiling salted water according to packet instructions.

2 Prepare the meat or seafood according to type, slicing meats finely. Heat the oil in a wok and add the garlic. Stir-fry for *1 minute* or until just golden. Add the meat or shellfish with the pepper and stir-fry for *4–6 minutes* until tender.

2 Add the rice sticks, vegetables, soy sauce, *nam pla*, sugar and egg. Mix well and cook for a further *3 minutes*. Firm vegetables, like cauliflower, require slightly longer cooking than tender vegetables, such as courgettes. Transfer the rice sticks to a warm serving dish and garnish with omelette slices.

Serves 4

Crispy Rice with Dipping Sauce

Preparation time: 5 minutes
Cooking time: 25 minutes

When boiling rice, Thai cooks reserve the layer of sticky grain left in the bottom of the saucepan to make this dish.

- 250 g (8 oz) glutinous rice
- vegetable oil for deep-frying

DIPPING SAUCE:

- 125 ml (4 fl oz) Coconut Milk (see page 9)
- 50 g (2 oz) minced pork
- 50 g (2 oz) peeled cooked prawns, minced

- 1 teaspoon Garlic Mixture (see page 9)
- 1½ tablespoons *nam pla* (fish sauce)
- 1½ tablespoons sugar
- 50 g (2 oz) onion, finely chopped
- 50 g (2 oz) roasted peanuts, crushed

1 Place the rice in a saucepan and pour in water to cover it. Bring to the boil, cover and cook until the rice is thoroughly cooked and sticky. Drain the rice in a sieve. Spread the rice out in a layer, as thinly as possible, on greased baking trays, pressing down well. Set aside to dry in a warm place or in an oven at 120°C (250°F), Gas Mark ½ (see page 7).

2 Meanwhile, make the dipping sauce. Pour the Coconut Milk into a saucepan and slowly bring to the boil. Add the minced pork and prawns, stirring to break up any lumps. Mix in the Garlic Mixture, *nam pla*, sugar, chopped onion and roasted peanuts. Reduce the heat and simmer the sauce for *20 minutes*, stirring occasionally.

3 When completely dry and firm, remove the rice from the trays with a spatula, breaking it into large pieces (see page 7).

4 Heat the oil for deep-frying to 180–190°C (350–375°F), or until a cube of bread browns in *30 seconds*, and deep-fry the rice pieces until golden. You should hear the grains beginning to pop in about *5 seconds*. Remove from the oil with a slotted spoon and drain on kitchen paper.

5 Pour the dipping sauce into a bowl and serve with the crispy rice pieces.

Serves 4

Chow Mein

Preparation time: 10 minutes
Cooking time: 5–8 minutes

- 500 g (1 lb) chow mein
  noodles
- 4 tablespoons vegetable oil
- 1 onion, finely sliced
- 125 g (4 oz) cooked pork,
  chicken or ham, cut into thin
  shreds
- 125 g (4 oz) mangetout or
  French beans, trimmed
- 125 g (4 oz) bean sprouts

- 2–3 spring onions, finely
  shredded
- 2 tablespoons light soy
  sauce
- 1 tablespoon sesame oil or
  chilli sauce
- salt

1 Cook the noodles in a large saucepan of boiling, salted water for *3–5 minutes*, or according to packet instructions. Drain and rinse under cold running water until cool. Set aside.

2 Heat a wok, then add about 3 tablespoons of the oil. When the oil is hot, add the onion, meat, mangetout or beans and the bean sprouts, and stir-fry for about *1 minute*. Add salt to taste and stir a few more times, then remove the mixture from the wok with a slotted spoon and keep it hot.

3 Heat the remaining oil in the wok and add the spring onions and the noodles, along with about half the meat and vegetable mixture. Stir in the soy sauce, then stir-fry for *1–2 minutes*, or until heated through.

4 Transfer the mixture from the wok to 4 warm serving bowls, then arrange the remaining meat and vegetable mixture on top. Sprinkle with sesame oil or chilli sauce (or both, if preferred) and serve immediately.

Serves 4

variation

Vegetarian Chow Mein

1 Prepare the ingredients as in the main recipe, substituing 1 finely sliced green pepper for the meat.

2 Continue as in the main recipe, adding 175 g (6 oz) each of shredded Chinese cabbage leaves and whole baby spinach to the wok *1–2 minutes* before serving.

Vegetable and Side Dishes

Palate-refreshing vegetables with seasonings to tempt the taste buds feature in this collection of lively recipes, bursting with texture and flavour. Stir-fried Ginger Broccoli or Spiced Cucumber would be ideal to enliven simple grilled fish, poultry or meat and some recipes like White Cabbage Salad or New Potato Curry star as innovative main courses in their own right.

White Cabbage Salad

Preparation time: 20 minutes
Cooking time: 10–15 minutes

- 300 g (10 oz) white cabbage, finely sliced
- 3 tablespoons vegetable oil
- 1 tablespoon sliced shallots
- 1 garlic clove, crushed
- 1 tablespoon chopped dried red chillies
- 1 tablespoon *nam pla* (fish sauce)
- 1½ tablespoons lemon juice
- 1 tablespoon roughly chopped roasted peanuts
- 4 tablespoons Coconut Cream (see page 9)
- 10 cooked king prawns, peeled, deveined (see page 8) and halved lengthways
- 250 g (8 oz) sliced roast pork
- salt

1 Add the cabbage to a saucepan of boiling water and cook over a high heat for *2 minutes*. Drain the cabbage in a colander, refresh it under cold running water, return it to the pan and heat through.

2 Heat the oil in a wok. Add the shallots and stir-fry for *2 minutes*, then, with a slotted spoon, transfer to kitchen paper to drain. Add the garlic to the oil remaining in the wok and fry over a gentle heat until just golden. Drain on kitchen paper as for the shallots. Cook and drain the red chillies in the same way, adding more oil if necessary.

3 Transfer the cabbage to a large bowl, add the *nam pla*, lemon juice, peanuts, Coconut Cream, prawns, sliced pork and salt to taste, then mix well. Spoon the salad on to a warm serving plate, sprinkle with the stir-fried shallots, garlic and chillies, and serve immediately.

Serves 4

Warm Thai Salad

Preparation time: 15–20 minutes
Cooking time: 15 minutes

- 6 tablespoons vegetable oil
- 12 spring onions, finely sliced
- 5 cm (2 inches) fresh root ginger, peeled and finely chopped
- 1 boneless, skinless chicken breast, finely sliced
- 2 tablespoons *nam pla* (fish sauce)
- 500 g (1 lb) cooked king or large prawns, peeled and deveined (see page 8)
- 1 tablespoon chopped flat leaf parsley, to garnish

HOT DRESSING:
- 2 red or green chillies, deseeded and finely chopped
- 2 large garlic cloves, chopped
- grated rind of 1 lime
- juice of 3 limes
- 2 tablespoons *nam pla* (fish sauce)
- 1 tablespoon soft brown sugar

SALAD:
- ½ head crisp lettuce, shredded
- 1 bunch radishes, finely sliced
- ½ cucumber, finely sliced

1 First prepare the Hot Dressing: grind the chillies in a blender or food processor along with the garlic and grated lime rind to make a rough textured paste. Alternatively, pound the ingredients to a paste in a mortar using a pestle. Stir in the lime juice, *nam pla* and sugar. Set aside.

2 Mix together all the salad ingredients in a serving bowl and set aside.

3 Heat a wok, add 2 tablespoons of the oil and heat over a moderate heat until hot. Add half of the spring onions and half the ginger and stir-fry for a few seconds to flavour the oil, then add the chicken and sprinkle over half of the *nam pla*. Increase the heat to high and stir-fry for *3–4 minutes* or until the chicken is lightly browned on all sides.

4 Remove the wok from the heat and transfer the chicken to a plate with a slotted spoon. Pour out and reserve any cooking juices from the wok. Stir-fry the prawns in the same way as the chicken, using more oil, with the remaining spring onions, ginger and *nam pla*. Remove the prawns from the wok and add them to the chicken with their cooking juices.

5 Heat the remaining oil in the wok over moderate heat, pour in the dressing and stir until it is hot. Replace the chicken, prawns and their cooking juices and stir to heat through and mix with the dressing. Pour the contents of the wok over the salad ingredients, toss to combine and serve at once, garnished with flat leaf parsley.

Serves 3–4

Okra with Tomatoes

Serve this lightly spiced vegetable mixture as an accompaniment to curries, or with simple grilled, fried or barbecued meats. Okra, also known as ladies fingers, have a flavour similar to aubergines.

Preparation time: *15 minutes*
Cooking time: about *12 minutes*

- 75 g (3 oz) clarified butter (ghee) or 25 g (1 oz) butter mixed with 2 tablespoons vegetable oil
- 4 green cardamoms
- 1 small onion, finely sliced
- 500 g (1 lb) okra, trimmed
- 500 g (1 lb) tomatoes, skinned and quartered
- 1 teaspoon garam masala
- salt and pepper
- 2 tablespoons chopped fresh coriander, to garnish
- poppadums to serve (optional)

1 Heat the clarified butter or butter and oil mixture in a wok and add the cardamoms. Fry these for a few seconds, then add the onion and a little salt and pepper and cook for about *5 minutes*, until soft but not browned. Add the okra and tomatoes, and cook for about *5 minutes*, stirring the vegetables frequently. The okra should be tender, but take care not to overcook them because then, in a fairly dry dish of this type, they can become slimy and unpleasant in texture.

2 As soon as the vegetables are cooked, sprinkle on the garam masala, garnish with chopped coriander and serve immediately with poppadums, if liked.

Serves 4

variation
Spicy Courgettes and Tomatoes

1 Substitute 500 g (1 lb) of baby courgettes for the okra and cook them as in the main recipe.

2 Serve with naan bread instead of poppadums as the mixture may be slightly more liquid and the bread will soak up the wonderful spicy juices.

New Potato Curry

The potatoes in this curry absorb the flavour of the spices and their texture and taste
are perfectly complemented by the tangy yogurt sauce. For a complete change, serve
this curry as the main dish and prepare a selection of side dishes to go with it.

Preparation time: 10 minutes
Cooking time: 20–25 minutes

- 50 g (2 oz) clarified butter
  (ghee) or 25 g (1 oz) butter
  mixed with 1 tablespoon
  vegetable oil
- 2 large onions, finely
  chopped
- 50 g (2 oz) fresh root ginger,
  grated
- 2 garlic cloves, crushed
- 2 bay leaves
- 1 stick cinnamon, broken in
  half
- 2 teaspoons fennel seeds

- 3 green cardamoms
- 1 teaspoon turmeric
- 1 kg (2 lb) small new
  potatoes
- 600 ml (1 pint) water
- 300 ml (½ pint) natural yogurt
- chilli powder, to taste
- salt and pepper

TO GARNISH:
- chopped fresh coriander
- 4 kaffir lime leaves

1 Heat the clarified butter or butter and oil mixture in a wok.
Add the onions, ginger, garlic, bay leaves, cinnamon stick,
fennel seeds, cardamoms and turmeric. Fry, stirring
continuously, until the onion is soft but not browned.

2 Stir in the potatoes, pour in the water and add salt and
pepper to taste. Bring to the boil and cover the wok. Simmer
for *10 minutes*, then uncover and cook fairly rapidly for a
further *10 minutes*, or until most of the water has evaporated.

3 Pour the yogurt over the potatoes and heat gently, to avoid
curdling the sauce. Sprinkle with chilli powder to taste before
garnishing the curry with chopped coriander and kaffir lime
leaves serving it with any of the following accompaniments.

Serves 4

ACCOMPANIMENTS

Peeled cooked prawns, sprinkled with a little grated lemon
rind and chilli powder.

Chopped cooked chicken, sprinkled with toasted flaked
almonds and chopped chillies.

Crisp bacon rolls – although not a typical accompaniment
for curry, they taste delicious with these potatoes.

Quartered hard-boiled eggs, sprinkled with a mixture of
paprika, a little chopped thyme and salt and pepper.

Peeled green and red peppers, chopped and sprinkled with
a little crushed garlic and oil. To peel peppers, hold them on a
fork over a gas flame, or cook under a very hot grill until the
skin is blistered, then rub off the skin under cold running water.

Wedges of cucumber, sprinkled with a pinch each of ground
cloves and chilli powder.

Quartered tomatoes, sprinkled with thinly sliced onion rings.

Indian breads and chutneys – for example, chapatis,
poppadums or naans, and lime pickle, mango chutney or
peach chutney complement the spices in New Potato Curry.

Sayur Kari

Sayur Kari is an Indonesian vegetable curry with fried beancurd and it is best served freshly cooked, with rice. If yellow beancurd is not available, use firm-textured beancurd as found in many supermarkets or wholefood shops.

Preparation time: 15 minutes
Cooking time: about 30 minutes

- 2 tablespoons vegetable oil, plus extra for deep-frying
- 4 squares of yellow beancurd, cut into 2.5 cm (1 inch) cubes
- 4 shallots, sliced
- 2 fresh green chillies, deseeded and sliced
- 3 garlic cloves, chopped
- 1 tablespoon finely chopped fresh root ginger
- 1 lemon grass stalk, finely chopped
- 1 tablespoon ground coriander
- 1 teaspoon ground cumin
- 1 teaspoon turmeric
- 1 teaspoon galangal powder (optional)
- 1 teaspoon chilli powder
- 1 teaspoon shrimp paste
- 600 ml (1 pint) Vegetable Stock (see page 9)
- 400 ml (14 fl oz) Coconut Milk (see page 9)
- 250 g (8 oz) potato, diced
- 125 g (4 oz) green beans, topped, tailed and cut into 1 cm (½ inch) lengths
- 125 g (4 oz) white cabbage, finely shredded
- 75 g (3 oz) bean sprouts
- 25 g (1 oz) rice vermicelli, soaked in boiling water for 5 minutes, then drained
- salt

1 Heat the oil for deep-frying in a wok to 180–190°C (350–375°F), or until a cube of bread browns in 30 seconds. Deep-fry the beancurd cubes in batches for about 1 minute, until they are crisp and golden. Remove with a slotted spoon, and set aside to drain on kitchen paper.

2 Heat the 2 tablespoons of oil in a wok. Add the shallots, chillies, garlic, ginger and lemon grass, and fry over a gentle heat, stirring frequently, for 5 minutes, until softened.

3 Add the ground coriander and cumin, turmeric, galangal powder, chilli powder and shrimp paste. Fry the mixture for 1 minute. Stir in the stock and Coconut Milk. Bring to the boil and add the potato. Reduce the heat and cook the potato for 6 minutes. Add the beans and cook for a further 8 minutes.

4 Stir in the cabbage, bean sprouts and rice vermicelli, season with salt to taste and cook gently for a further 3 minutes. Stir in the fried beancurd and serve.

Serves 6

Braised Aubergines

Preparation time: 15 minutes
Cooking time: 7–10 minutes

- vegetable oil, for frying
- 4 spring onions, sliced
- 4 garlic cloves, sliced
- 2.5 cm (1 inch) fresh root ginger, peeled and finely sliced
- 2 large aubergines, cut into 5 cm (2 inch) strips

- 2 tablespoons soy sauce
- 2 tablespoons dry sherry
- 2 teaspoons chilli sauce

GARNISH:
- 1 red chilli, deseeded and chopped
- 1 green chilli, deseeded and chopped

1 Heat 2 tablespoons of oil in a wok. Add the spring onions, garlic and ginger, and stir-fry for about *30 seconds*. Remove the mixture from the wok and set aside.

2 Increase the heat, add the aubergines and stir-fry until they are browned, adding more oil as necessary. Using a slotted spoon, remove the aubergines and drain on kitchen paper.

3 Pour off the oil from the wok. Return the spring onions, garlic, ginger and aubergine to the wok. Add the soy sauce, sherry and chilli sauce, stir well and cook for *2 minutes*.

4 Spoon the aubergines into a warm serving dish, garnish with red and green chillies and serve immediately.

Serves 4–6

Stir-fried Vegetables

Preparation time: 10 minutes, plus soaking
Cooking time: 3–4 minutes

- 5–6 dried shiitake
  mushrooms or 50 g (2 oz)
  button mushrooms
- 250 g (8 oz) Chinese leaves
- 175 g (6 oz) carrots, peeled
- 125 g (4 oz) French beans,
  trimmed
- 4 tablespoons vegetable oil
- 1 teaspoon salt
- 1 teaspoon sugar
- 1 tablespoon light soy sauce

1 Pour warm water on the dried shiitake mushrooms, cover and leave to soak for *25–30 minutes*. Drain them and squeeze dry. Discard the hard stalks and finely slice the mushrooms. If using fresh mushrooms, just wipe and slice them.

2 Cut the Chinese leaves and carrots diagonally into thin slices. If the French beans are small, leave them whole; if they are long, cut them in half.

3 Heat the oil in a wok and add the Chinese leaves and carrots. Stir-fry them briskly for *30 seconds*.

4 Add the beans and mushrooms and continue stir-frying for *30 seconds*. Add the salt and sugar, then toss the vegetables until well mixed. Stir in the soy sauce and cook for *1 minute* further. Transfer to a warm serving dish and serve immediately.

Serves 3–4

Stir-fried Spiced Cucumber

Preparation time: 10 minutes, plus standing
Cooking time: 5 minutes

- 1½ cucumbers, peeled
- 2 teaspoons salt
- 1 tablespoon oil
- ¼ teaspoon chilli bean sauce
  or chilli powder
- 6 garlic cloves, crushed

- 1½ tablespoons black beans,
  coarsely chopped
- 5 tablespoons Chicken Stock
  (see page 9)
- 1 teaspoon sesame oil
- cucumber slices, to garnish

1 Slice the cucumbers in half lengthways, remove the seeds and then cut the flesh into 2.5 cm (1 inch) cubes. Sprinkle them with the salt and leave to drain in a colander for about *30 minutes*. Rinse in cold running water, drain well and dry thoroughly on kitchen paper.

2 Heat the oil in a wok, then add the chilli bean sauce or chilli powder, garlic and black beans and stir-fry for about *30 seconds*. Add the cucumber and toss well to coat the pieces with the spices. Pour in the stock and continue stir-frying over a high heat for *3–4 minutes*, until almost all the liquid has evaporated and the cucumber is tender.

3 Transfer to 4 warm serving dishes. Sprinkle with sesame oil, garnish with slices of raw cucumber and serve immediately.

Serves 4

Stir-fried Ginger Broccoli

Preparation time: 10 minutes
Cooking time: 3 minutes

- 2 tablespoons vegetable oil
- 1 garlic clove, finely sliced
- 2.5 cm (1 inch) fresh root
  ginger, peeled and finely
  sliced

- 500 g (1 lb) broccoli, divided
  into florets and sliced
- ½–1 teaspoon sesame oil

1 Heat the oil in a wok, add the garlic and ginger, and stir-fry for *2–3 seconds.* Add the broccoli and cook for *2 minutes.* Sprinkle the sesame oil over the broccoli, adding sufficient to suit your own taste, and stir-fry for a further *30 seconds.*

2 Spoon the cooked broccoli into a warm serving dish and serve immediately.

Serves 4

variation
Chilli and Ginger Broccoli

1 Cook the garlic and ginger in the wok as in the main recipe, and add 1 deseeded and finely chopped red chilli.

2 Continue as in the main recipe and serve hot on a bed of steamed rice or tossed with some cooked egg noodles.

3 Garnish with thin strips of red chilli, if liked.

Special Photography:
Sean Myers
Jacket Photography:
Front Jacket: Peter Myers
Back Jacket: Sean Myers
Recipe Photographers:
Octopus Publishing Group Ltd./
GGS Photographics,
Sandra Lane, James Murphy,
Peter Myers
Home Economist:
Sunil Vijayakar